BE THE
SECOND COMING

Also by Hope Ives Mauran
Where the Wisdom Lies: A Message from Nature's Small Creatures

Emotional Transformation: Learn to Speak the Language of Creation
(audio CD)

BE THE SECOND COMING

*Guidebook to the Embodiment of the Christ Within:
A Personal Journey, Our Collective Destiny*

HOPE IVES MAURAN

BALBOA.
PRESS

A DIVISION OF HAY HOUSE

Balboa Press books may be ordered through booksellers or by contacting:

Balboa Press
A Division of Hay House
1663 Liberty Drive
Bloomington, IN 47403
www.balboapress.com
1-(877) 407-4847

Because of the dynamic nature of the Internet, any web addresses or links contained in this book may have changed since publication and may no longer be valid. The views expressed in this work are solely those of the author and do not necessarily reflect the views of the publisher, and the publisher hereby disclaims any responsibility for them.

The author of this book does not dispense medical advice or prescribe the use of any technique as a form of treatment for physical, emotional, or medical problems without the advice of a physician, either directly or indirectly. The intent of the author is only to offer information of a general nature to help you in your quest for emotional and spiritual well-being. In the event you use any of the information in this book for yourself, which is your constitutional right, the author and the publisher assume no responsibility for your actions.

Any people depicted in stock imagery provided by Thinkstock are models, and such images are being used for illustrative purposes only.
Certain stock imagery © Thinkstock.

ISBN: 978-1-4525-3663-7 (e)
ISBN: 978-1-4525-3662-0 (sc)
ISBN: 978-1-4525-3664-4 (hc)

Library of Congress Control Number: 2011911270

Printed in the United States of America

Balboa Press rev. date: 8/25/2011

The reference point and destination for this guidebook is heaven on earth, the earth that existed before the fall from grace.[1] The possibility of this world to exist now would not be within my awareness if it were not for the writings of Baird T. Spalding, the author of *Life and Teaching of the Masters of the Far East.*

In deepest gratitude, I dedicate this book to
Baird T. Spalding
and to the masters
who have lived and continue to live in this way.

Acknowledgments

Thank you to all who have helped to create this book: especially Martha, for your encouragement in helping me to get past the early hurdles I encountered and for your presence in my life in so many ways; Mary, for your inspiration, guidance, and connection to that which inspires action;. Alana, for walking beside me, tactfully editing, and learning the meaning of the words with me … we went deeper together than would ever have been possible alone.

To those who read and commented, my sincerest appreciation for your insights and suggestions: Elise, Emily, Lisa, Ellen, Susie, Maria, Ariel, Avis, Susan, Darla and Maria Gabriella.

To Michael, for your companionship, comments, encouragement, and the many amazing breakfasts.

To Fred, Elise, Rall, and James for your steady support and love throughout the time of transition for us all.

To Craig Hamilton, thank you for the Evolutionary Life Transformation Program that has faultlessly moved in step with my journey of writing the book. Words cannot describe how your work has guided, and encouraged this book into form.

And lastly, thank you to all the representatives of the vast unfolding mystery: the One. You have assisted in ways I can't even imagine and at levels that I have no knowledge of! I am honored to sit here as scribe. Namaste. We are one.

CONTENTS

List of Illustrations

Encounter with Jesus
New York Times Headline

Please Note
The words and messages of the guides and Jesus are in set off from the text and/or noted as such. The words in square brackets have been added for clarity.

The term "Man" is capitalized and is used for all humans, both women and men.

The terms "All That Is," "God," "the Divinity," "the Source," and "the One" are used throughout interchangeably. "Goddess" is inherent within these energies, as is "God." These terms encompass all separations.

BOOK 1

CHRIST CONSCIOUSNESS IS POSSIBLE

PREFACE

This book is an invitation to see the world and your own potential in a completely new way. The rather bold title, *Be the Second Coming*, invites the Christ to return. And indeed, that is what this guidebook offers—not in the form of a new messiah but in the form of the messiah that lies dormant deep within you. The risk in reading the book is that you may experience a total change in your frame of reference. You may come to realize that all the powers Jesus demonstrated lie inside you! In truth, you are the living Christ; we all are. The bridge to allow access to such a gift is the lens of unity consciousness or seeing "all as one." The consciousness of Christ sees all as one. In seeing yourself and everything around you as an extension of yourself, you enter the kingdom of God, and the world becomes a completely new place.

This is not a religious book written for Christians but rather a book about the essence all humanity shares. It is a book for people of all faiths and paths. Please don't let the word "Christ" keep you from this treasure. "Christ" is simply a title that means "one who embodies God." All people carry the same inner spark of God and may find this guidebook to be useful for the journey to the Christ within. It's like a Fodor's Travel guidebook, with all the information you need to guide yourself on an internal journey to your Christ self. This book will describe what your Christ self is, what is needed to bring it out in you, what it changes in your life, and how to recognize its presence in your life. This book even includes guidance on what to "unpack" and leave behind in order to express your inner Christ, because your inner Christ is something you uncover; there is nothing you can add to yourself to get to it.

This guidance was gifted to me so that I could share it with you. Jesus Christ himself offers this guidance; I have simply translated it into words. I offer my conversations with Jesus here, conversations I have in my head in the same way that I speak to my spirit guides or my higher self. I hope their grace will touch you in your journey through these pages.

The writing process has been transformative for me. Each time I have edited, the landscape has become more clear and thus, becoming the Second Coming has become more possible. In rereading this book, I have found deeper meaning and more ways to recognize, access, and empower this part of myself. In sharing the stories that I have included, I have realized that I had expressed the Christ within myself all along; I just hadn't used the word *Christ* before. I hope that as you journey through these pages, you too will recognize the Christ that you are and have been all along and be further opened to freeing its power to transform your life and the world we all share.

There is a distinguishing difference of meaning between Jesus and Christ. His given name was Jesus; his honorific title was "Christ." In his little human body called Jesus was born the vast Christ Consciousness, the omniscient Intelligence of God omnipresent in every part and particle of creation.[2]
—Paramahansa Yogananda, *The Yoga of Jesus*

1. HOPE'S JOURNEY

April 21, 2008, I was naked and lying face down on a massage table when Mary, my friend, a spiritual healer and massage therapist, whispered softly in my ear, "You made a commitment before you even came to earth. You committed to embodying the Christ consciousness, and the time for it to come into fruition is in the next five years." A flash of recognition came to me. *Oh, of course!* I thought as I breathed a sigh of relief. You know that sensation when something that you feel but haven't been able to find words for is finally spoken? An underlying tension that I had held forever dropped; I didn't even realize I was holding that tension until I let it go. It was replaced by a feeling of peace. I got up from the massage table and dressed as usual, but something had shifted. Truth was present almost like another person had entered the room.

I had been wondering where my spiritual journey would lead. Having read over a hundred spiritual books, I was searching for *something* and never would have dared to call it "Christ consciousness," which sounded religious and out of reach. Mary had been offering me guidance whenever she came to town, and many really transformative and wonderful things had resulted. So, I trusted her clarity and her source. I took her words seriously and committed myself to fulfilling that pre-birth pledge and discovering for myself just what it meant! Not surprisingly, my ego, that part of me that loves to separate itself from others by being special, liked the lofty goal. So, like bringing an unruly friend on a delicate mission, we set off on this quest with a destination that only the truest parts of me would complete.

⤳

The words "Christ consciousness" were like a beacon of light guiding me ahead during a confusing period of my life. They offered a hopeful vision and destination, because a year earlier my decade-long, almost insatiable thirst for spiritual understanding and wisdom had precipitated a move to the country. I moved alone, without my husband and youngest son, which seemed selfish and foolhardy to some of my friends and family. Others admired my courage and willingness to take a spirit-guided leap into the unknown.

I had been caught in a painful dance between leaving and staying, I was unhappy staying and scared to leave. I felt like I had one foot on the dock and one in the boat, and the boat was drifting away from the dock—I didn't know what to do. The marriage was not serving my husband or me, and I was unable (or unwilling) to find another solution. As I drove over a rise one day and saw the cliffs on the Shawangunk Ridge ahead of me, my guides said to me, "There's home." But I didn't get it. The second time they said it, a few weeks later, I was able to hear and feel it. I decided to find a house and move, as that second call ended up being the pull I needed to move out of my indecision and inertia. I was moving away from my married life and the dream and security that it once held, but what was most excruciating was that I was leaving my youngest son, as well.

It had become more and more difficult to fit myself inside the definition of "wife." Although I still loved my husband and didn't want to hurt him or our three children (two of whom were off at college), a part of myself was dying. It became clear that the only way I knew to save myself was to dissolve the marriage—or, perhaps more accurately, complete it. In addition, I didn't like who I had become when I was with my husband, entrenched emotional patterns held me captive and I didn't know of any other way to move out of them. Reluctantly, I moved beyond the marriage, but toward what, I had no idea.

Shortly thereafter, a new man came into my life, orchestrated deftly by the guides, (and amazingly supported by my husband.) He brought an opportunity for healing on many levels and yet created even greater irreconcilable extremes in my life.

And so I found myself living in the country in a house near the end of the cliffs, while my youngest child stayed with his dad one and a half hours away. This allowed my son to remain at the school he loved and in a familiar neighborhood where he had friends. It was extremely difficult; I wanted to be there for him as I always had been, but I knew that modeling for him being true to my spiritual self was also a gift in some ways. The theme of separation, the need to reconcile two irreconcilable realities, was everywhere in my life. My old life was broken in pieces, and the vision for my new life was hazy and didn't fit into any molds I was familiar with. Isolation and humility are perfect incubators for transformation. My retreat to the literal and proverbial "wilderness" left me feeling like I was in free fall with no floor or walls to define my world. It was terrifying and freeing at the same time, and it forced me to live in the moment; to look forward toward the future or back at the past were too painful. I kept a Louis L'Amour quote on a card by my kitchen sink, and it gave me a hopeful shift in perspective many times. It said, "There will come a time when you believe everything is finished. That will be the beginning."

Difficult times can offer great gifts on a spiritual level. I shed many layers of conditioning with regard to my expectations, obligations, and assumptions about what was most important. Seeing life through society's eyes simply didn't work anymore. Society's values alone didn't take into account my spiritual longing and whatever it was that was calling me. Being on a spiritual rather than a religious path, there was no obvious way to accommodate that calling. For months and years after my move, I tried to figure out how to put my life back together, to make the people I loved happy and be happy myself. But it was like trying to put together a jigsaw puzzle that simply didn't fit, and it made me crazy.

The situation eased considerably when I finally realized that accepting life as it is (as opposed to resisting it) gave me peace and allowed me to find the gifts in the form that my new life had taken. Surrendering, I gently hit bottom and was then able to settle into a new and more balanced perspective. Instead of focusing on what I didn't have, I realized what I did have. I had deep alone time *and* time with my son, family and friends. I had always needed time alone, but I hadn't known how to balance my own needs with the needs of the children and the nurturing of the family.

Nature's beauty and healing energy supported me and reminded me of life's sacredness. I reconnected with the land, which helped me to feel connected to everything around me. Nature gave me the opportunity to see the unity of all, even in the anguish of separation that felt so real. A saving grace was that I was mostly able to understand the ups and downs I was going through as just part of a process I was in, and I felt my only choice was to hang on and try to enjoy the ride.

⌒

So this is how I found myself two days after my massage with Mary, sitting in bed around 4 a.m. with my laptop on a pillow, heeding a call from my guides or the Divinity within me. They asked me to take a half hour each day to allow the "wisdom that flows through me" to express itself on paper, and they gave me this title for a book: *Guidebook to Christ Consciousness: A Guidebook for the Transcendence of Human Thought Patterns and the Movement Out of the Prison of the Illusion That We Are Simply and Only Individuals in a Physical Realm and to the Truth of our Unity, Our Oneness Beyond the Physical Evidence, and the Transformation to the Resurrected Christ, as Demonstrated by Jesus.* How's that for a mouthful of a title?

My guides were asking me to co create a guidebook, like a manual for the planting of vegetables or the assembling of an elaborate toy. I had to get over my incredulity that I could actually do this and proceed. Knowing that I was essentially just the scribe at first made the task manageable, yet just opening to "the wisdom that flows through me" didn't result in the structure or substance of a book. I also realized that inherent in the assignment to write a guidebook was the need to demonstrate the Christ within myself. With that not insignificant pressure, my confidence eroded, and I stopped writing.

⌒

A year after the guidebook assignment, I remembered that tucked away in a binder were the written records of a miraculous series of meditations that I had had ten years before. It was in 1999 that my guides first helped me to embody the Christ, so I realized that I *already had* embodied the Christ! The memory of what it felt like to be the Christ from the inside made me realize that the Christ is indeed within me; "the divinity within" me was real, not just words that I wanted to believe. I knew them as Truth. This gave me the courage to begin writing again.

After my embodiment of the Christ, my guides took me to see Jesus, so I knew he existed and that it was possible to converse with him. I also had another experience with him that I illustrate below, so I knew he wasn't just a lofty historical figure, but a real presence.

When my son, James, was about two, I was pushing his stroller down a country road in Rhode Island. A car came barreling down the two-lane road toward us, never shifting toward the center as most cars do when they see a pedestrian. I shoved the stroller off the road into the underbrush, got off the asphalt, and turned to scowl at the driver, exclaiming, "Jesus! #!*%!" under my breath. As I watched the car go by, in my mind's eye I saw Jesus, his arms through the roof of the car, his body streaming out behind, and his hands holding the steering wheel! His head was turned toward me, and he was smiling as if to say, "Nothing to worry about; you're safe." I was transported instantly from fear to joy. I felt so taken care of!

The book changed again when I realized that I could also speak to Jesus directly to ask him to define Christ consciousness and the path to getting there. I offer my conversations with Jesus here, conversations I have in my head, in the same way that I speak to my guides. Who am I to speak to Jesus personally? It wasn't something I set out to do. Yet, my spirit's commitment to embody the Christ energy has forced me to release my sense of unworthiness to do such a thing. I am no one special. However, I have learned to attune in a way that allows these words to come through. I feel quite certain that all of us have gifts, and being a channel is one of mine. Perhaps it is through giving life to our gifts and talents that we all open to express our Christ within. The Christ energy is present within all of us; our inner Christ is the truth of who we really are, if only we can allow it to be. In accessing this part of ourselves, perhaps we also awaken others to the Christ within themselves.

Through meditations that my guides taught me to do in which I modeled the unconditional love of Christ, I caused something in the heart of another human in Yugoslavia that impacted the physical world. So the guidebook continues with this story of Christ embodiment. Upon the first hearing, the story may seem fantastic, but imagine what is possible when we allow the Christ or Divinity that we truly are to express itself through us. Before I can share the story, first I need to tell you about Shadrach.

2. SHADRACH

"We are not human beings having a spiritual experience; we are spiritual beings having a human experience." This familiar quote by Pierre Teilhard de Chardin became true for me in 1998 when I learned how to converse with Shadrach, a nonphysical guide and teacher—the older, wiser spiritual aspect of my physical self, my Divinity within. He had always been *in my head* somehow. The name Shadrach had been floating through my awareness for as long as I could remember. He inhabited my thoughts and had all my life. So, teasing his individual presence from the matrix of my mind was a profound transition that opened up a brand new world to me. We conversed (sometimes on the computer and sometimes just in my head), and my world cracked wide open, expanding to the size of the universe. His answers were clear and made sense and radiated with unconditional love. He gave me advice on many subjects, exhorting me, "Life waits for no one to be a better person tomorrow. Whatever your plans for change and evolution, charge ahead with them."

Unfortunately, I wasn't able to do all that Shadrach suggested. Though he was filling my mind with wisdom and encouragement, I rarely found the focus or will to put it into practice for more than a few seconds at a time. I realize now that this was because channeled words have a specific quality of energetic vibration that speaks directly to our spirits. Our lives, however, are mostly not run by our spirits. A changing stream of selves with differing needs and wants (our minds, hearts, bodies, egos, training, inner wounded children, and so on) run our lives, and they are all of different vibrations. The spiritual journey is the process of getting all parts of ourselves on the same vibrational frequency and aligned to a higher purpose. For me, this is like trying to train a ragtag army into a unified force that acknowledges the spirit's authority.

Shadrach affirmed the magic of earthly life for me: "There is always meaning in things if you search for it. Your life will be filled with joy and emotion to a dizzying extent." With this knowledge, the world around me became a conscious, living being, infused with loving connections and communications. My heart opened to the birds, trees, and flowers, and they began to convey messages. I felt my intuition strengthen and magic return to my life, which my traditional education and reliance on science alone had so effectively dulled. Before my spiritual awakening, I had been one of the "I need to see it to believe it" folks. As I opened to the spirit's presence in my life, my heart opened. I found myself crying at the simplest things, such as the beauty of sunlit dewdrops on the grass or a story in the newspaper about people helping others.

Shadrach encouraged me to slow down, to be more present, and to use my time in a different way. I learned to be still, both physically and internally, more than I ever had before. One theme reappeared often: "The best thing for you to be is *joyous*."

"I will try," I replied, "but sometimes it is a struggle to find that place of joy."

"The place you will find it is within, not without. Go within. Be quiet in yourself. Make time for prayer and concentration. Make time to be still and sit in wonder of the web of life as you have come to know it. This will help you find your joy."

I realize now that joy opens up communication with our divine selves, and that's really the whole point! This was counter to what I was taught. In my puritan heritage, the focus was on duty. Joy wasn't spoken of or valued for the potent energy that if brings to life.

All Life Is One

One day, as I was driving, I asked why so many animals were killed on the road. Shadrach said that they were offering themselves as a reminder that they are present in the land and that they wish to be considered when we do things that affect them. I wished I could help them to convey this message more succinctly![1] It was also a relief to hear that the animals had chosen to die in that way! Afterward, instead of feeling sad when I saw a furry lump on the road, I felt a surge of gratitude for each animal's communication to us and its ultimate sacrifice. I wanted to honor the animals, so I asked what I could say that would do that. Shadrach said, "All life is one. May you be blessed." I say that whenever I pass an animal on the road now.

Shadrach's words enabled me to see beyond the seemingly harsh physical evidence of life to a purposeful perspective in which I understood that things were happening for a reason. It gave me a lighter perspective about life and also helped me to realize that from the vantage point of our spirits, death is an illusion. Our bodies may die, but there is a part of us that continues to live on. Adding the dimension of the nonphysical to my world gave me more choices about how to respond to life, and my perspective shifted from seeing earth from close up to seeing her from a greater vantage point. The change gave me an intense awareness of the bigger picture being enacted on earth while also opening my heart and causing tears to flow whenever something that expressed our unity came to my attention.

The time I spent in communication with Shadrach allowed me to consider the invisible world around me. It became evident to me over time that the world we see is just a fraction of reality. Simply

---

1   In recounting this story, I realized that my first book, _Where the Wisdom Lies: A Message from Nature's Small Creatures,_ does precisely this!

hearing his explanations about things and experiencing the expansion of my perspective that Shadrach engendered made me see how blind I had been. There was so much more to this world than I had ever imagined! I realized that everything is connected—everything! And the repercussions of that were mind boggling. If everything is connected, then it is all *one thing*.

I wanted to feel connected to that *one thing*, but like most people, I was circling around the creations of the One, the Divinity, and what I craved union with it. I wanted to be in sacred connection with everything around me: the trees, the grass, the people—the teapot, even. And to do that, I had to look from *inside the center*, as though I were wearing God's spectacles! So I wrote notes and pasted them around my home to remind me that said, "God's perspective in all things."

Looking from the perspective of the One or the Source, I became part of it. From *that* place, the feeling that I had searched for was present. Experiencing wholeness from inside of the Source makes you feel whole. Try it. When I finally saw this, it reminded me of searching everywhere for my glasses and finding them on my head!

An Exercise for Seeing All as One
Take an object that you are near right now and imagine that it is a part of *you*. See its essence as the same as your own. Focus on *that which is the same in everything* as you look at it. Remember the illustrations in school of electrons circling an atom and all of that empty space between the electrons? That empty space is the same in everything. Can you soften the definition of who you are and expand it to include the object? Then try it with something else and then again with something else. Then include the whole room—know that the items and spaces are *you*. Can you observe a change in how you feel and how you relate to everything else when you do this? (Additional exercises in appendix A will help you to expand the definition of who you are.)

Training for a New Kind of Work: Sowing Seeds of Love

Shadrach's perspective was expansive: "Disassociate yourself with the human condition and think only in terms of the universe." I did find I had a predilection for seeing the big picture, and when I did, I realized how the details of daily life seemed uninteresting. A few months after I began formally communicating with Shadrach, he intimated that a big change was coming in our work. I could never have dreamed possible what lay ahead. On April 7, 1999, I received this from him:

> I want to talk to you about your visionary journeying. It is something that you will be doing more of as time goes on, and my hope is that you will find it … educational and enjoyable. The way for you to start is to envision yourself high above the stars so that you can see down to the surface of the earth. You will then try to see and imagine the blockages that are part of the system of earthly energy. The earth is a very changeable place; she can be warm or cold, happy or disrupted, and much of its state is determined by the status of her energy flows.
>
> You have the capability to affect the earth's energy blockages through your meditation. It is hard to believe and imagine, perhaps, but it is true. You must think of yourself as a person of great power and potential impact, for you can make a difference on a global level. You must start by seeing the earth from above. Envision areas of strife and discord like Bosnia, and then work within yourself to open those areas. You can do this by envisioning joy and brotherhood between enemies. You can do this by sending light and energy to the people in these places who are being hurt and terrorized. The possibilities are really endless.

The earth's energy and its flow affect how the people living upon her feel and act. When the land's energy is blocked, I imagine it is like having a pebble in your shoe, a low-level irritant. When it is flowing and harmonious, the people who live there feel more at ease. That would explain why certain parts of the earth have been in turmoil repeatedly throughout history. Shadrach trained me to see where the energy flow of the earth was blocked and to remedy it. We humans are only aware of a fraction of our capability to create!

I would wake up very early (between 4 and 6 a.m.), before my children got up, and sit cross-legged on the floor, leaning against the bed with my laptop in my lap, and do meditations that Shadrach trained me to do. When I got up to start my day later on, I felt like all my "work" for the day was complete. Everything else paled in comparison to the satisfaction I felt having completed those meditations in the morning. The contrast was marked. From feeling like I could never get enough done in a day, I shifted to a peaceful knowledge that all was perfect, and *nothing* more was needed. This feeling was of *true* work well done. It satisfied me deeply.

3. THE MEDITATIONS

Shortly after we began doing the meditations together, Shadrach became quite urgent, trying to get through to me the importance of what I was being asked to do: "You must understand the global impact you can have if you can harbor your energy to allow its allocation for this end. All that you have done up until now has been preparation for the *real* work that needs to occur *now*. This may seem melodramatic or urgent to you, but it is true. Imagine you have *five months to live*, and in that time, you must *save the world* through your meditation. It is that important. Live it, breathe it, be it, enjoy it. You find the time and the energy, and I will guide you."

His statements *were* rather fantastic. He even wanted me to get a chauffeur to drive the children so I would have more time and energy for this work! Who could you tell this stuff to? Nevertheless, I did try to find more time and take it seriously. I didn't go into the experience expecting to see the results of the work confirmed; I did it simply as a willing student.

Balancing the Earth's Energy Flows

In the spring of 1999, I practiced in earnest the series of meditations or visualizations for the earth that Shadrach had been exhorting me to do, wondering if they really would have an effect. I soon saw that they did. The energy flow within the earth affects how people feel and act upon her, and conversely, people's actions affect the energy of the earth.

In 1999, there was turmoil in the Balkans. Slobodan Milosevic, president of Yugoslavia (as reported in the *New York Times*) had "been central to four consecutive Balkan wars—in Slovenia, Croatia, Bosnia and now Kosovo—over the past eight years."[2] There were 740,000 ethnic Albanians forced to leave their homes in Yugoslavia, along with stories of mass killings and brutality. In late March, NATO forces had been bombing the country in an attempt to oust Milosevic and his Serbian Army. On April 1, I began meditating on the earth in Yugoslavia from my home in Connecticut.

If you could imagine you were a satellite circling the earth or that you had a view from the moon, you could perceive that an energy blockage on the earth was contributing to this destructive situation. War after war, neighbor killing neighbor ... that is not how you would think people would choose to live. One reason that people act this way is because of the earth's energy beneath their feet. It also has to do with their patterns of (often shortsighted) behavior or the behaviors of their ancestors that set destructive processes in motion.

In my meditations, I was able to balance the earth's energy flow by visualizing that I was high above the earth, looking down upon her From that perspective, I could see the distant land and somehow also the energy movement within it. Where it was blocked, I freed its flow by finding what was blocking it (sometimes deep in the earth) and removing it. I did this repeatedly, always assisting the energy of the earth to flow at a suitable rate, neither too fast nor slow, and to distribute the energy to those areas that had not been reached. As

---

2   Cohen, Roger. "Crisis in the Balkans: Overview; Warrants Served for Serbs' Leader and 4 Assistants." *New York Times*, May 28, 1999.

energy flowed to areas without it, the energy was absorbed like water into thirsty land. It was a relief that I could literally feel.

I could see the change that occurred in the land as I worked on the energy flow each day. I removed red rocks from blocked energy arteries, and the flow of energy to those areas increased and brought immediate relief. The areas felt and looked very different from the rocks around them, and removing the rocks was like removing splinters. Over time, the land relaxed. When I didn't know how to remedy the situation, I would ask for guidance. I prayed over the land, loved it, radiated warmth to it, broke up hard crusts on it, and did whatever else it called for.

All of this occurred as I sat on my floor in Connecticut, typing out what I was doing on a laptop. Anchoring myself in the physical action of typing kept my mind from wandering too much.

Milosevic Meditations
As the land relaxed and the energy flowed smoothly, I was directed to visit the people living on it. I first balanced the earth in the Kosovo area on April 24, which is when I began visiting and blessing Slobodan Milosevic, then president of Yugoslavia. I started visiting many others on May 1, a week later. I acted from faith, knowing that what I was doing was beneficial on some level. And that was enough; expecting to see results seemed unlikely.

I did not know then what scientists have been discovering about a field of energy that connects everything and acts as a medium of communication. Numerous researchers are documenting the phenomenon of being able to affect someone "nonlocally and virtually instantaneously."[34] So, what I did for the earth, and later with people, now seems quite possible even though it seemed to be a big stretch at the time.

Over a period of five months, I balanced the earth's energy and visited Slobodan Milosevic in meditation, interacting with him in my mind's

---

3   McTaggart, *The Field*, 25.

eye. I developed a relationship with him within the meditations. I never met him in person. There was an openness and eagerness present in him after my first visit. It felt like his heart opened. Here are excerpts of what I typed that day:

Shadrach: I would like for you to go to Kosovo this morning. Look down on the earth as you have done before. How is the energy flowing?

Hope: Fine through the mountains, and the plains seem to be covered, too.

Shadrach: Okay, now take yourself down to the village you first visited with me.

Hope: I walk into the town. Children and dogs see me and run to me as I walk. People gather around ... I lay my hand on each of their heads, saying, "May the Lord's light shine down upon you and your family always. May you find peace, love, compassion, and joy. May you know happiness and love of your fellow man. May you know of God's power through you and of your power to create your world."

I leave there to see ... a headquarters area, where people in charge sit around a conference table. They look at me in disbelief. They are afraid to acknowledge me. I move from one to the next as they continue their work. I bless them each in turn. It is with this blessing that they become humane again. They bow their heads and weep. At last I get to the leader (I believe this is Milosevic). I do the same for him, and then I touch him on his heart and ask for forgiveness for his actions, that he may forgive himself and that others may find it in their hearts to forgive him. I ask that he become an instrument of peace and love throughout his land. He doesn't wish to acknowledge me, but he sees and hears me and feels my words. I envelop him in a beam of golden light and ask for God's energy to heal him of his hatred. He stands proudly for a moment and then finally bows his head and cries. I leave there and move on.

Shadrach: You have done much today. This is of much greater import than you know. These people and Milosevic are touched in a place that needed touching. This is an important day for this country.

Each day, I visited Milosevic on the stage of my mind's eye. We had conversations, but mostly I just loved him truly and completely, without judgment. It wasn't that I *refrained* from judging—I couldn't judge him, because I loved him unconditionally. I accepted him fully, and my heart was open to him. The love I emanated was a kind of power that flowed through me; the words were just a part of what occurred. It seemed that its power was able to dislodge things in its path that were unlike itself; its divine origin was unquestionable. I prayed over him as someone giving a benediction or blessing of grace—not as a petitioner. I heard his concerns and counseled him.

The *I* who visited him was not the everyday Hope. It was a self that I had not been before. I was like Christ. It was without pretension or walking in shoes that I couldn't embody truthfully. I *was* truly this energy, and I said to myself, "I sound like Jesus!" But the amazing thing was I *felt* like Jesus, as well! With Shadrach at my side, the transition to embodying the Christ self in the meditations was not only possible; it was natural.

On May 8, 1999, a breakthrough occurred when my conversation with Milosevic indicated a change of heart.

Hope: I have an urgency to be with Milosevic this morning. I find him in the same room, talking strategy with his leaders. I go directly to him first. He smiles when he sees me.

Milosevic: Ah, so it is the great spirit again. I am doing the things that you tell me, but I am getting stuck. What am I to do now?

Hope: Follow your heart. May your heart be full of love for Man in all ways. May you have compassion, love, understanding, and courage to do the work that you know and feel must be done. May your way be clear to a new understanding of life, living, and the world around you. May your people support you in this work. May your knowledge of God grow in all things and in all ways.

Milosevic: My heart says to stop, but what do I tell my people?

Hope: You tell them that your heart tells you to stop, to make amends to those you have wronged. You say you are led to this because of your love for them and their children and your fellow human beings. Remember, you are the leader. They follow you because you have led them by thinking for them in many ways …

Milosevic: Thank you. I will try.

Hope: You will succeed, because you have love behind your words and actions. That is the key.

I embrace him. I touch all of those people around him, pray for them, and ask that they support their leader in his decisions based on love.

Results!

After a "regular" meditation on June 3, Shadrach took me to a field of flowers in colors I had never seen before. I stood in front of a bare-chested man with a powerful yet gentle presence; he was sitting in a wooden chair. It later dawned on me that the man was Jesus. At the time, I just knew that the man was a leader.

Jesus said, "You will see the impact of your work very soon; keep watching the newspapers for your confirmation of all of this. It is imperative."

Later as Shadrach and I parted he said, "That is good, my dear. There is no more for you to do today. Watch the newspapers as we have told you."

I interacted with Milosevic daily and with refugees, villagers, soldiers, resistance leaders and others in towns and cities throughout Yugoslavia. The energetic *I* (sometimes many of them) went to those places in my meditations. Visiting Milosevic taught me that interacting on a nonphysical plane of existence could affect behavior at the physical level. Perhaps being opened to love made continuing on the path he was on no longer tenable because it was so out of alignment with the love he now felt. I don't have answers to the question of how this works, but the results were in the news.

The front-page banner headline of the *New York Times* on June 4 , 1999 announced: "Milosevic Yields on NATO's Key Terms; 50,000 Allied Troops to Police Kosovo."

I was elated and knew a miracle had occurred. I thought to myself (and out loud to the few friends who knew of this work), "I'm not crazy! It really worked!" I think I walked on air for several days after that, feeling an inner warmth and joy, knowing *something* that I couldn't put into words but that felt so right and real and good. The following day I was taken again to the field of flowers in colors that don't exist on earth to speak with the man I now knew as Jesus. He helped me to understand why I had that indescribable *knowing* when he said, "Trust the world that you have experienced now in this wonderful and mysterious way. This is the world to trust and share as your own."

The mysterious *something* was that in truth the world is so much more than I had ever been taught. Some part of me now knew that miracles were not impossibilities; they were true responses to an undiscovered higher law.

After this evidence that I was connecting to physical reality through meditation, I continued as before, balancing the earth and visiting Milosevic and the refugees. It felt like the number of refugees was endless, and I had been asked to meditate twice a day because the need was so great.

Much later, I sought proof that what I had experienced really happened, and I read the articles that mentioned Milosevic at that time. Prior to my visits, Milosevic was adamant about not allowing allied forces into the country, and his change of mind came right at the time when I first met with him. Even though the Reverend Jesse Jackson, a Baptist minister, had visited him around that time, it was quite clear from the communications with Jesus and the guides that my meditations were critical to Milosevic's change of heart. After his announcement, the State Department, the Pentagon, and the White House expressed "skepticism" and "surprise" that Milosevic was authentic.[4] It was also reassuring to note that Milosevic's behavior had changed as well. He was described as "calm" and respectful, in contrast to a previous visit.[5] Not only had Milosevic surprised the West with his major shift, but he was also acting differently enough for it to be reported in the newspaper. It appeared he had become more balanced, just like the land.

I continued with the work for many weeks after that with an increased sense of wonder at the seeming miracles of this earthly life. I accepted them, but I didn't know how they were possible from a physics standpoint. Looking back to that time now through the lens of a unified whole, my simple explanation is that we are all one in a huge vibrationally choreographed dance. A miracle is simply cause and effect, like the One, All That Is, itching in Yugoslavia and calling Connecticut to scratch it.

---

4   Erlanger, Stephen. "Milosevic Yields on NATOs Key Terms: 50,000 Allied Troops to Police Kosovo." *New York Times*. June 3, 1999.

5   Harden. "Crisis in the Balkans: Doing the Deal—A Special Report: The Long Struggle That Led Serb Leader to Back Down." *New York Times*. June 6, 1999.

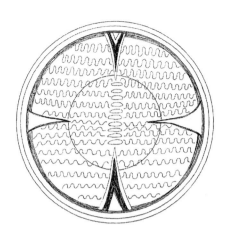

4. EXPLAINING THE UNEXPLAINABLE

How could a person meditating in Connecticut change events in Yugoslavia? It seems to defy our understanding of the world, our training, and our logic. And yet science is now confirming the unity of our world and the potential to affect things remotely.

Many researchers have shown the power of human intention to affect plants, animals, bacteria, yeast, isolated human cells, and enzymes. Not only that, but a reproducible experiment is that a group of people can affect the breathing and eye movements of another group of people from far away.[6] There are different theories on how this is possible. Yet, regardless of the explanation of *how* it is possible, there is proof that it *is* possible.[7]

6   McTaggart, t*he Field, 133.*

7   *The Field: The Quest for the Secret Force of the Universe,* a book by Lynne McTaggart, compiles the research on the phenomenon of the energy that connects us all. After reading a book such as this, the idea that you can affect another person far away through the power of unconditional love will seem logical and almost obvious. Hal Puthoff, a laser physicist, explains the Zero Point Field (ZPF) as a

     'kind of self-regenerating grand ground state of the universe', which constantly refreshes itself and remains a constant unless disturbed in

These scientific studies offer strong evidence to support a different view of what we are capable of and the degree to which we unknowingly affect each other all the time. The potential to touch another person, be they nearby or far away, through unconditional love is even greater. The evidence of our interconnectedness is compelling. I know this now. But at the time of the Milosevic meditations, I was challenged on many levels to believe that our interconnectedness was possible.

Shadrach offered encouragement: "I wanted to talk to you about the way things are going for you. You are having trouble with your sense of reality in regard to your channels and meditations. This is understandable, because it is so foreign to you. But one thing you must realize is that people have been doing this sort of thing for a *long* time. It is just that you didn't know about it."

---

some way. It also means that we and all the matter of the universe are literally connected to the furthest reaches of the cosmos through the Zero Point Field waves of the grandest dimensions. page 25.

It appeared that the Zero Point Field creates a medium enabling the molecules to speak to each other nonlocally and virtually instantaneously. page 68.

Marilyn Schlitz and William Braud did a study with two groups of people, One nervous group and one generally calm group. The calm group was able to calm the nervous group down remotely. The "need" for calming that the nervous group exhibited created a statistically significant result. It meant that other people could have almost the same mind-body effect on you that you could have on yourself. Letting someone else express a good intention for you was almost as good as using biofeedback on yourself. page 132.

They compiled research conducted from all over the world that had shown that human intention could affect bacteria and yeast, plants, ants, chicks, mice and rats, cats and dogs, human cellular preparations and enzyme activity. Studies on humans had shown that one set of people could successfully affect the eye or gross motor movements, breathing and even the brain rhythms of another set. The effects were small, but they occurred consistently and had been achieved by ordinary people who had been recruited to try out this ability for the very first time. page 132-133.

Imagine my delight when I then discovered *Alien Dawn: An Investigation into the Contact Experience*, a book by Colin Wilson. It blew me away. It talks about people meditating in hotel rooms throughout the world to avert the assassination of Yassar Arafat at a press conference, thus averting a Middle East war that would've escalated into a world war! It sounded to me like maybe I wasn't crazy, as there were others out there doing this!

Anastasia's Ray

Further confirmation of the phenomenon is found in *Anastasia*,[8] the first book in the *Ringing Cedars* series. The series tells the story of Anastasia, who lives in a remote taiga of Russia as naturally as the animals who serve her and bring her food. She has no house, wears little clothing and lives as part of the natural world. This may conjure up a vision of a heathen, but her mastery on all levels is astounding and encouraging, because she demonstrates the highest human potential. She is able to see the past and knows what is going on all over the world without ever leaving her woods!

What struck me like a bolt of lightening when I read it—I burst into tears—was the use of her "ray." By focusing on the inner plane, she is able to open a line of communication allowing her to remotely view and assist people from a distance. She demonstrated this by looking in on the author's wife from hundreds of miles away. Anastasia asserts that the ray can gather or transmit information, cheer up a mood, and help heal depending on the user's energy, will, desire, and degree of feeling. The overriding condition critical to controlling the ray is the purity of the user's thoughts and the strength of their radiant feelings.

Anastasia's ray is not unlike what I used in the Milosevic meditations. The purity of thought that she says powers the ray could be termed "unconditional love." What is more pure than a love that wants to open a heart to healing and love with no thought of return or payment? The engine of both her ray and the Milosevic meditations is focused and radiant unconditional love. The context that makes all

---

8   Megre, *Anastasia.*

of this possible is the unity of the world we live in and our hearts' connections to it.

Life and Teaching of the Masters of the Far East

The most inspiring and transformative books that I have read are the six-volumes of spiritual classics by Baird T. Spalding in which he describes a group of scientists' travels during several trips to Tibet, India, and China in 1894. They met and traveled with spiritual masters, documented their abilities, and conveyed their teachings. They met Jesus as a living being in a human body, who like other masters could appear miraculously, one of the books quotes Jesus referring to a ray, as well. "You can transform God-power and send it out with such force that it is irresistible. These are the beams or rays of light that you see emanating from my body. These rays are emanating from your body, although they are not yet as potent; but as you go on and use this power, allied with Law and Principle, you will add potency to the light and can consciously direct it to accomplish any good desire."[9]

Confirmation from other sources that this kind of work was possible was a joyful revelation. Anastasia and the masters do this, and their message is that we, too, are capable of it. We all have the capacity to focus our thoughts with intention and open our hearts to assist the world. This is just one of our divine inheritances. Our every emotion, thought, action, and word is creative. Conscious use of these energies in alignment with our divine selves can create "miracles."

We Are Born Creators

The divinity that shapes your destinies is not a mighty person molding you as a potter molds his clay but a Mighty Divine Power—within and all around you and around and in all substance—which is yours to use as you will.

—Spalding, *Life and Teaching of the Masters of the Far East.*

---

9   Spalding, *Life and Teaching*, vol. 3, 34.

The truth is that we are creating whether we want to or not. The energy we put out into the world draws like energy to itself, forming more of itself. So what is the mechanism by which this creative communication occurs?

Resonance and Harmonic Resonance

Resonance and *harmonic resonance* may explain the phenomena of instantaneous remote and inter-dimensional communication.

Resonance occurs between things of like vibration. For example, mothers and children, identical twins, or lovers can sometimes feel each other's emotions, thoughts, or situations when they are apart. This occurs through their shared vibration and their bond—it's like they are tuned into the same radio station. Additionally, resonance could explain why sometimes when you think of someone, he then calls you on the phone. It is a powerful force that draws together harmonious components in our world.[10]

Harmonic resonance is resonance that reaches inter-dimensionally. There are dimensions of reality (other than this 3-D one that we live in) that exist within different ranges of vibration on a continuous scale, vibrating at a higher or lower rates. Perhaps our musical scale is a section of that continuous scale, because harmonic resonance is best described through music. For example, when a C note is struck on a piano, all the other C wires in the piano will start to vibrate even though they haven't been touched.[11] Similarly, our vibration on earth affects other dimensions, perhaps because the continuous scale of vibration is like the musical scale in how it responds. Imagine flicking a light switch and having it turn on lights that illuminate scattered trees in a huge park. Harmonic resonance is like that, with the distant trees being other dimensions instantly affected by us.

Joy, gratitude, and love resonate with like energies and dimensions, thus expanding the presence of these beautiful qualities in our lives and world. It naturally follows that when we vibrate at a place of

---

10   Karim, Biogeometry Lectures, November 2009
11   Ibid.

frustration or struggle, those vibrations creatively expand into the world, as well.

When I asked Jesus to expand on this, he said, "When one strikes a note on earth, it is heard throughout the universe—not only in the divine dimensions, but in all places and levels. For this reason, there is no way to constrain the effect of what we do on earth. Not only does this offer us a conduit to higher worlds and potentials, but it also means that our *every action and word* is harmonically shared and thus introduced into the soup of universal existence. So when we become aware of our actions, thoughts, and manners of being on earth, we become blessings as opposed to the alternative! Our vibrational offering is seeding our energy and our entire lives into the fiber of the universe. When this is known, and *one attains a practice to ameliorate the extremes of earthly life*, it is a great blessing. Namaste. We are one."

Scalar or compression waves can explain Jesus's amazing statements. They are standing wave forms that some scientists theorize create the substrate within which all resonance occurs. They are a form of sound and vibrational waves that have a "memory." Compression waves result from movement. They are analogous to sound waves, but their effects are instantaneous and persistent: they continue on and on. A boat moving through the water, sound through air, electricity through a wire, and spoken words all create scalar waves.[12] The universe is filled with them; constantly moving at all levels of creation.

It is not a huge leap from here to realizing the connection between our every action, thought, word, and emotion and the profound and lasting impact each makes throughout the universe. Perhaps this explains how the register of our every action and thought is available to those who can "read" it (as in the Akashic Records),[13] and how we, individually and as a collective, have created the difficulties we are

---

12 Ibid.
13 Akasha is a term that means "air" or "ether." It is used to describe a record of all things that have occurred, a record that is accessible to those in deep hypnosis and present within the "air" or "ether." See "Akashic Records" at Wikipedia, *en.wikipedia.org/wik/akashic_records,* for further information.

facing now on earth. We live in a vibrational soup and cannot control where our vibrational touch goes, which means that our loving and our destructive thoughts are ever present in the universe!

Dancing with the Universe

I remember one evening turning on some music in my office; oddly, I didn't recognize the CD that was playing. I started dancing with reckless abandon. I love to dance. I thought to myself, *I am dancing all alone*, but then I realized in a lucid instant that no, that wasn't possible; I was dancing with the *entire universe*. I froze in mid movement, smiled, and welcomed the universe in as we danced on.

In that instant, I realized that whatever I was *offering* in any moment was what the universe was receiving! Knowing there is a factor of infinite expansion in action in the universe is a really clear incentive to clean up my emotional act! One of the practices I have taken up as a result of my dance is to "monitor my offering" to the universe. It reminds me of a message from my guidance: "Offer only unto the present moment that which you hope to receive in the next moments—for eternity."

Resonance, harmonic resonance, and compression waves are some ways to explain how we are dancing with the universe all the time. I wanted to hear what Jesus would say about the permanence of our actions and asked him, "Jesus, is there a memory of the harmonic relationships and of our thoughts, emotions, and actions, as well?"

Jesus answered, "Yes, of course there is. No matter what occurs on earth and in the hearts of men, there is a record of it. Not only in the ethers but also in the very neurology of the individual. This is how a happy person looks youthful and vibrant and an angry person is wizened and taut. So it is the vibrational signature that holds matter in form. And that is also why matter and our bodies are flexible and changeable. We may reconfigure at any time what our body looks like by redefining or representing a different vibrational signature. What often occurs is that people don't realize the power of their thoughts and … they continue to dwell upon those things that don't support their true desires in life. Their thought vibrations then manifest or continue in the physical form. So your true work is to lighten up your thoughts, and all else will follow."

I have seen firsthand how my inner vibration affects how I look. When I love and am connected to my spirit and happen to look in a mirror, I am astonished by how young I am. And when I am joyful and openhearted, I find people respond in that way, too. We are creating our bodies and redefining our worlds one moment at a time, one thought at a time, and one choice at a time, leaving a record of what we have created and reaching places we had no idea even existed.

Knowing that the thoughts of unity and feelings of unconditional love that access Christ consciousness are the same as the ones that assist us to create consciously can help us navigate this new territory. There is a special quality of energy that emanates from us when we pray, bless, love, or consciously connect with nature. It is the same energy found in sacred places and healing wells[14]—*and in divine dimensions.*

Unconditional Love in Higher Dimensions
I once stumbled into the divine nonphysical world by "chance." I was lying on my bed in the early evening. I'd taken a shower and was very relaxed. I was practicing a breathing technique I had just read about[15] when strong tingling began at my feet and enveloped my body upward. It was a pleasant and intense feeling. When it encompassed my whole body, a veil lifted. And all of a sudden, like a channel change on TV, there were the heads of two old men in profile, bathed in bright light. I was filled with unconditional love, something I had no memory of having ever experienced before. It felt so good, but these words fall short of conveying its depth. Telepathically one of them said, "Oh, I can't believe you are here so soon!" I thought, *Oops, what have I done?*

---

14 Karim, Biogeometry Lectures, November 2009.
15 Epstein, *The 12 Stages of Healing*, 39-40.

and then simply basked in the love, not wanting it to end. Now I wish I'd thought to ask a few questions!

Afterward, in my delightful confusion, I wondered, *Where was I?* and *If that was God, why were there* two *of them?* It was only later that I realized that I had stumbled into the afterlife and that there are many spiritual guides assisting us behind the veil in nonphysical dimensions. They guide our journeys in response to our intentions, thoughts, desires, emotions, and requests for help. Unconditional love was the quality of the dimension that I opened to it was radiant and filled me completely.

In radiating the unconditional love of the Christ, we speak the same language that the creator speaks—and this is where the fun begins!

Manifestation

Remote effects like the Milosevic meditations are just the tip of the iceberg of what we are capable of. I hope I don't send you over the edge into disbelief, but in vibrational alignment with divine energy from the Source, we are not only powerful creators over distances but can manifest our physical needs, such as food, shelter, safety, water, and even wine! It seems impossible, yet there are people who demonstrate such things.[16]

Manifestation is not your usual conversation topic among friends and family! Most people don't believe that we have this potential, and this lack of belief creates its own limitation; when you think you can't, you can't. To manifest, you must know it is possible. It is available not from the outer world but from the inner world; the inner world projects the outer world into being. You must therefore go inward to manifest as the Christ.

---

16 Wright, *Behaving as If the God in All Things Mattered*, 141–142.

Truly knowing something comes only from personal experience. It is from *knowing* that you are a creator, that the Christ or God power lies within you, that your life may be transformed and a new world becomes possible. *You must claim this knowing for yourself,* because no one else will bestow it upon you.

BOOK 2

GUIDEBOOK TO THE CHRIST WITHIN

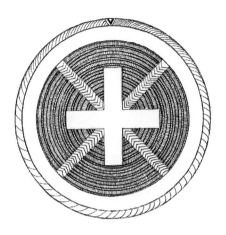

5. WHAT IS CHRIST CONSCIOUSNESS?

Knowing that embodiment of the Christ is possible, I ask Jesus, "What is the full manifestation of Christ consciousness?"

Jesus answers, "The Christ self is indwelling and eternal, as it exists in manifest expression through the living human form—not only as a human being but also as a God incarnate. The potential [to embody the Christ] lies in all incarnated humans. The Christ self is … one who has allowed the truth of 'what is' to express itself fully without interference or distortion on the level of the human. Namaste. We are one."

So, the Christ self is quite simply one who thinks, speaks, and acts from within the oneness of everything, one who knows the unity of all and doesn't let human perspectives and imperfections interfere with or distort this vision. When we are our finest selves, we are the Christ. This can manifest in the smallest act, such as preparing a simple meal, or in the grand heroic act of one who risks her own life to rescue a stranger's. The thread that runs through any act done as the Christ is its genesis from *within* the unity and love of all. The Christ self manifests as the cook, as Christ has a joyful reverence for the foods as they are prepared and shared, and as the rescuer, as Christ values the life of another as much as the other values his own.

So the "truth of what is" that Jesus speaks of in his definition is the reality that there is just *one* divine process in this world, and we are all a part of it. The plants, the animals, the very earth herself, the space between us, the stars, the moon, and the galaxies that exist beyond our sight are all only *perceived* as many. In seeing others as yourself, your self's boundary is burst open, and your heart connects to all that it sees. The realization that we affect those around us and that they affect us, all of a sudden requires us to be responsible to a much greater world.

Seeing All As One Changes Everything

I find that the simple awareness of this connection to and love of all things changes how I feel in any moment of my life. Walking in a crowd of people and focusing on *what is the same* within us all can make me relax and smile; I feel completely different about myself and everyone else. Several years ago, I was sitting on a bench in the middle of the woods, just looking at the trees. In an instant, the trees changed from being things that were outside of myself to being my friends; I saw each of them as individuals. It completely changed being in the woods. I think many of us fear the woods, because we hold the memory of the danger that hid within them for our ancestors. All vestiges of that fear dropped from me in that moment, as the trees became my family of protectors instead. Perhaps you can see how seeing all as one changes everything.

The difficulty lies in allowing this truth of our divine light and love to express itself "without interference or distortion." Most of us cannot see this truth of our unity—and understandably, because it is not visible to our naked eyes! Add to that the fact that our minds are busy, our bodies are tense, and there have been a gazillion generations of humans on earth living in the same blindness!

One thing that can support us in turning our focus inward to discover the Christ within us is when we become still of mind, relax our bodies, and enter a state of allowing. Then we can make space for the God within us to manifest through us. Just knowing that this magnificence of divine Christ light is within us can allow us to free it from its jail! It doesn't have to take great time and effort (although it may) to free the Divinity within us to express itself through our lives, bodies, and hearts.

Even now we can recognize that the Christ self has been here all along. Perhaps when we speak a truth we didn't even know we knew, that is the Christ within us using our voices. Or the Christ may be acting through us when we feel no limits to what is possible for ourselves or for others—when we humbly feel like "God incarnate." (Humility is a key to action as the Christ, for that action comes from the knowing that I am but a part of something magnificent and beyond comprehension.) The Christ may be acting through us when we move outside of our comfort zones and speak a hard but necessary truth. Or maybe the Christ is acting through us when we reach out to a stranger to make a loving connection beyond the bounds of social norm.

My friend Avis inspired me with her story of how she responded to beggars when she and her family lived in London. Knowing the men asking for money might spend it on liquor, she instead invited them to eat with her and her children at a restaurant. The men would sit with them or at another table—whatever they wanted to do. She could see her unity with them and openheartedly was willing to act on it way outside the normal social boundaries. This is Christ in action.

Having the definition of Christ consciousness, the next question might be, "What must one do to get there?"

Here is the conversation that Jesus and I had about this:

> **Jesus**. The first and only step is *the Intention to be one with* all life, all things seen and unseen. From this vantage point,

43

all actions, all thoughts, and all intentions are of the Christ consciousness.

When the Christed self evolves, there is a difference, however, as it evolves into a true embodiment. I believe this is what you are asking for, as are many others.

Hope: How?

Jesus: Focus on the realization that all is one. And whatever action you take must be action that serves the One in the largest sense. Your focus must be singularly held on the unity of All That Is as often as you are capable. Not only will this change your way of being in the world, but also it will ease the way for all of those around you, as well. You will still *do* the things you do, but you will simultaneously know that you are connected to all and, therefore, that your actions are responsible to the whole in a new way.

Jesus later added, "Seeing the One, All That Is, around one at all times is the simplest and most easily performed task that most people can practice. It can be done anytime, any place, anywhere, without anyone knowing it is being done. And it has profound effects on the nervous systems, both sympathetic and parasympathetic, and the systems that connect one to the higher dimensions. All barriers between the worlds are blasted apart when this frame of reference is used to see out from human eyes."

So, a new Christ intends to be one with all life, and a true Christ takes action that serves the One in the largest sense because she feels responsible to the whole.

Stop reading for a moment and shift your perspective to see everything in front of you as *all one thing*. Join everything together, and imagine the space between things as a "thing," as well. When I stop writing and shift to see that the wall, the table, and the map on the wall all are part of the same thing, I see that they are all the One thing. And I say to Jesus, "When I did that, everything came alive, conscious, and my body relaxed." And I find myself loving what I am looking at.

Hope: Am I relaxing because I am in resonance with the things I see as the One?

Jesus: No, you are not in resonance. You are connecting with them in a way that offers an opening to energy within your body system. You are in a working relationship with the earth when this occurs. You join a team made up of the universe, the earth, life forms, and other forms and exchange with them in a way that eases you. It brings the universe's wholeness to you and so you find yourself feeling whole.

Hope: Is this because I have stopped putting energy into being separate, as well?

Jesus: Not exactly. There is simply a union that occurs when you are looking at All That Is as a part of yourself, and that union taps into a deep well of that "who-you-truly-are-ness" that you don't normally feel. It is within you and available all the time. It is a contrast because you have not known to go there before!

As I embody the One, I feel more whole, not just in my perspective but in my body and emotions, too. New possibilities become available.

An Intimate Experience of Oneness
I was blessed to experience the world's oneness during a guided meditation by Sadhguru Jaggi Vasudev. I rose, and my first step on the earth was a shock because I *knew* the earth was alive. I couldn't walk normally because I felt so in love with the earth beneath my feet. I walked slowly—each foot placed lightly, gently, and painstakingly, as if I were walking on the face of something I loved completely and couldn't bear to harm. The tears poured down my face as my love for the earth moved through my body. It probably took me thirty minutes to walk about sixty steps; I had no reference for time. As people

walked around me to the door of the meditation hall, I felt deep remorse for my having walked, like them, clomping along unaware of the miracle beneath my feet. I was sensing that my body was a part of the earth herself. I reached and navigated the door at my snail's pace and saw the people, grass, and trees from a distance, they were all *one thing*. I knew them and myself as literally one thing.

It is so easy to forget that we are already the Christ; we don't need to *acquire* it. We are all the divine process in living form. In order to make the Christ within a real experience in our lives, we must let go of our idea of separation and of all the toys, costumes (masks), and tools that we have collected thus far that help us remain separate and that we imagine keep us safe. What remains is the truth of who we really already are: God incarnated as a human, openhearted and connected to everything else that is. When we see the world as one, we have the energy of a nuclear reactor within us, while as separate individuals, we sputter along on a generator as our only power source!

The Veil of Forgetfulness

My intention to embody the Christ is something that excites and inspires me, yet I forget constantly! I realized that it wasn't just that I, personally, was forgetful; forgetfulness is the human condition. One of the "terms," if you will, for incarnating in a human body is that we forget that we are one. Our journey on earth is to remember who we really are *in the body*. When we remember and see all as one, this knowledge feels like it would be impossible to forget, because it is so amazing. And yet, we forget again and again.

In seeing all as one, we are lifting the veil of forgetfulness. The veil is like an incredibly heavy theater curtain with thick layers of fabric and weights in the bottom: a huge curtain that separates us as humans from the truth that we are one. So we needn't chastise ourselves for forgetting that we are one, because it is not that we are imperfect in our ability. It is rather that it is challenging to go against the very rules of human birth. In order to play the game of appearing separate, we needed that curtain. When we see all as one, we are lifting the curtain up.

We expect ourselves to be able to hold it up all the time, but it is almost impossible—and even more so when we try to lift the veil alone. So as more of us remember our unity, we raise the curtain together, and the brilliant light beyond the veil shines out. If we share the job of lifting the veil together, we can remember our unity for longer periods of time, and more light and unconditional love will enter our world, reminding us that we are more than "just human"; we are the embodiment of God, come to earth as creators.

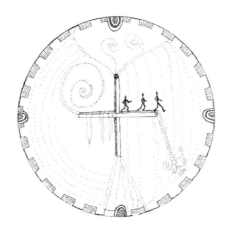

6. DATE WITH UNITY

Incredible as it may sound, we are actually *scheduled* to embody Christ consciousness as part of a preordained divine plan. This knowledge may embolden us to move toward it without fear of failure or fear of being the only Christ around! Several evolutionary models illustrate an active path to Christ embodiment—these may be described with different terminology, perhaps, but clearly our Christ selves are freed from their prisons within us, embracing the world as themselves.

The Mayan Calendar

The Mayan calendar describes a grand cosmic plan to achieve higher consciousness on earth. It charts fourteen billion years of life on earth from single celled organisms to human life in 2011![17] According to the Mayan prophecy, the cosmic winds are at our backs, moving us in the direction of unity consciousness with or without our awareness that it is happening. Dr. Carl J. Calleman's book, *The Mayan Calendar and the Transformation of Consciousness*, chronicles the schedule of creation and evolution.

---

17   The end date, according to Dr. Calleman, is October 28, 2011.

The ancient Mayans lived knowing the schedule of humanity's evolution, and thus they aligned with it in their daily actions and were able to use it to predict the trends of the future. Calleman explains that "thinking takes place outside of our bodies, essentially as part of a group mind of sorts," so our actions and thoughts are a result of "an evolving cosmic consciousness mediated by the earth, whose various energy shifts are described by the Mayan calendar."[18] He essentially is saying that this evolution is happening outside of our personal plans as a preordained evolutionary process.

Humanity's collective state of consciousness has developed *new levels of ethical behavior.* The Internet has created a powerful medium for transparency and increased integrity. At the same time, our compassion for our fellow humans and animals has become more widespread. The outpouring of generosity in widely publicized natural disasters like the tsunami in Indonesia or the earthquakes in Haiti and Japan are symptoms that illustrate a movement toward equality and openheartedness toward people we don't even know; this is tantamount to a collective expression of love and would have been impossible before this shift in how we define our realm of influence and responsibility.

According to the Mayan calendar, the evolution to *integrity* completed March 2, 2011 or thereabouts, after which *a new cycle began.* The new cycle is the evolution toward *co-creation* and *unity consciousness.* This, like the other levels we have experienced, is characterized by an acceleration of time (twenty times faster!), in which it will seem that more occurs in less time. This will no doubt translate into challenges for everyone. The new cycle initiates a major shift in how we see the world and ourselves. Our shift in perspective is a natural result of the occurrences, (like earthquakes and tsunamis) that demonstrate its truth. We are evolving to see our interconnectedness, which is followed by seeing the world as part of ourselves. We can no longer separate ourselves, because it becomes increasingly evident that the fate of all of us rests upon each of us, and the choices we make individually, as nations and as a collective. This change in

---

18   Calleman, *The Mayan Calendar,* xix.

perception occurs organically as a result of a rate of change that is almost impossible to comprehend, and the evidence that supports this expanded view of the world that we see on the front pages of the newspaper. We are no longer untouched by what happens on the other side of the world.

This change will be overwhelming to those who insist on interpreting life through the logical mind, or the left brain. We must add another tool to our "how to operate on earth" toolbox by becoming capable of turning inward to access the intuition and guidance of the right brain. The balancing of the right and left sides of the brain, and their female and male characteristics, will bring us to a whole and unified way of being on earth.

New awareness of the interconnectedness of all, an awareness centered in the right side of the brain, brings us to balance. This precipitates changes in how we wish to live, to be governed, to educate our children, to live in community, and to be in relationship. Systems and structures based on hierarchy and dominance will no longer have support in the new cycle, because they are not in alignment with the unity consciousness developing at this time. They will be replaced by a new vision of the earth as a conscious-unified world of interconnected beings that are responsible to the whole. Those structures, people, and ways of being that are out of synchrony with this shifting vibration will be set aside or will simply fall apart as the world that created them disintegrates.

The problems we experience today (environmental, social, governmental, and personal) are so many that our apparent powerlessness is overwhelming. While the situation may seem dire, a chaotic crisis actually can *assist* our transition to Christ Consciousness if we see the bigger picture. As the world's situation overwhelms our logical minds, it forces us to turn elsewhere for guidance; through necessity, we check for *internal* guidance, which is the direction in which we will discover and move a step closer to the Christ or God within.

We are then more willing to rely on our internal guidance and intuition to direct us toward conscious co-creation, creation with our Divinity within, in order to maneuver through life. We are scheduled to move into a *co-creative relationship* with our higher selves. What this means is that we will no longer make decisions solely based on our individual views and experiences.

Most of us have heard of the Mayan prediction of the world's end in 2012. I see this as the evolution of humanity to Christ consciousness through co-creation. Co-creation starts with freeing ourselves from our egos and surrendering to our higher selves. This must occur for the Christ within to find room for expression. So, the "co" in co-creation is the teamwork of the human self (and selves) and the Christ self. This is not possible unless we move beyond seeing ourselves as victims in the world or even as lone creators. The empowerment of this way of being comes from the awareness that all is one. Our role on earth is to offer through surrender the vessel of the body for divine expression on earth. It is what we came to do, and I can say from personal experience that *nothing* that I have ever done is more satisfying.

The degree to which we can move easily forward, before and after 2012, without resistance as the world changes will determine the earth's direction in the years ahead. Being aware of the greater picture helps us surrender to the process in action. If we can see the chaos around us as a healthy symptom that is necessary for changes to occur, our journeys take on new meaning. Our roles and responsibilities as holders of a vibration of unity and love and as creative visionaries become clear. When we see the earth around us and ourselves going through the slightly messy process of transition, we can experience optimism and courage instead of fear. By creating new structures, systems, and relationships that are aligned with this new worldview, we find that the world is reborn.

This time on earth is earmarked for significant shifts in human evolution and consciousness. The Mayan calendar outlines a grand cosmic plan that completely supports our embodiment of Christ consciousness; in fact it is pushing us in that direction.

> *The purpose of enlightenment in our time is not just to transcend the world, but to* transform *the world. How do we transform it? Through the evolution of our own consciousness. We have to realize that this process completely depends on us, on individuals who are willing to push the edge of the possible.*
>
> —Andrew Cohen, spiritual teacher and founder of EnlightenNext

So, you might wonder if there is any evidence of this consciousness on earth right now. Are there any people out there who are seeing the world around them as part of themselves?

Spiral Dynamics

The Spiral Dynamics model of human evolution suggests there may be. Spiral Dynamics offers a spiral representation of humanity's different vMemes ("vee-meems") or "levels of mind." VMemes describe the organizing principles in human nature: self and consciousness, brain-centered function, societal structure, environment, culture, and worldview.[19] Each vMeme has a (seemingly arbitrary) color to describe it. For instance, beige is biology driven ("I survive"), purple is group driven ("I am safe"), blue is obedience to a higher authority ("we are saved"), green is humanitarian, spiritual emergence ("we become"), etc.

The turquoise vMeme describes a "one for all and all for one" principle in which one acts for the good of the whole, and the whole picture is observable on all levels, including nonphysical dimensions. Only 0.1 percent of the human population is in this vMeme at this time. A tiny morsel of humanity, perhaps, but its mere existence means it is possible and will no doubt grow.

---

19 Beck and Cowan, *Spiral Dynamics: Mastering Values, Leadership, and Change.*

A Modern Day Christ

A recent NPR story described a man who was mugged at knifepoint by a teenage boy. The man gave the boy his wallet and then, as the boy left, offered him his coat and invited him to come have dinner with him! He said, "If you're willing to risk your freedom for a few dollars, then I guess you must really need the money." So they went to the diner where the man was a regular, and everyone there greeted him warmly. The boy remarked, "You are even nice to the dishwasher," evidently astounded by the man's way of being with others that was so kind and caring. When the bill arrived, the man said, "Look, I guess you're going to have to pay for this bill, 'cause you have my money, and I can't pay for this. So if you give me my wallet back, I'll gladly treat you." The boy returned the wallet, and the man gave him twenty dollars. The article ended with the man's quote: "If you treat people right, you can only hope that they treat you right. It's as simple as it gets in this complicated world."[20] This story illustrates Christ in action, demonstrating the turquoise vMeme and its "one for all and all for one" perspective.

The Yoga Sciences

The Mayan calendar offers a framework for the evolution of humanity from a cosmic level. The yoga sciences do a similar thing from the perspective of the human body. Regardless of their condition, our bodies are a miracle. No human designer or modern computer could create a system that works as exquisitely as our bodies do. We are the perfect manifestation of the creator, and we were made with the intention that the human body would offer God, the consciousness of the Christ, a dwelling in the physical realm. The yoga sciences assist the body's evolution and transformation so that it can hold the higher energies that being a house for God requires. Yoga is the science of the physical evolution toward enlightenment, awakening, and realization (or Christ consciousness) that has been practiced for thousands of years in India.

---

20 Garofalo, "Morning Edition," National Public Radio.

> *All life is evolving and man is no exception. Human evolution, the evolution which we are undergoing relentlessly, both as individuals and as a race, is a journey through the different chakras.*
>
> —Swami Satyananda Saraswati

The yoga sciences utilize the body's seven chakras to power human spiritual evolution. The chakras are energy centers aligned along the spine that receive, interpret, and transmit energies from the outer environment. They are like windows in the body.

According to Neil S. Cohen's *Chakra Awareness Guide*, "The energy created from our emotions and mental attitudes runs through the chakras and is distributed to our cells, tissues and organs. Realizing this brings tremendous insight into how we ourselves affect our bodies, minds and circumstances for better or worse."[21]

Our own thoughts and emotions, as well as the thoughts and emotions of others, go right inside us, and we translate them into our physical bodies. Perhaps this is why the bodies of saints and spiritual masters do not decay after death; their thoughts, devotion, and openness to the divine transfer high levels of spiritual energy into every cell of their bodies. And this, too, helps us to see that our bodies and our influence really don't end where we thought they did.

The gasoline for the engine of spiritual evolution is kundalini, a powerful energy that is coiled at the base of the spine, like a snake. Sadhguru Jaggi Vasudev says one only becomes aware of it *once it begins to move*.[22] Each chakra starting from the base of the spine and moving upward is awakened by the catalyzing energy of the kundalini shakti.[23] *Shakti* is a word that comes from the Sanskrit *shak*, meaning *to be able*, and *ti* is *the agent for all change*. The chakras are each

---

21 Cohen, 1.
22 Sadhgura Jaggi Vasudev is a Yogi, mystic and master. Who teaches Isha Yoga.
23 Cohen, 1.

associated with different functions, emotions, organs, and levels of awareness.

The *first* chakra, or root chakra, is located at the base of the spine. It is associated with survival and connection to the earth, and it gives vitality to the human body. Once the first chakra is awakened, we are freed from fear around our survival as individuals.

The *second* chakra, or navel chakra, located in the lower abdomen, rules our assimilation of food, sexual expression, desire, giving, receiving, and creativity. As it is awakened, we transcend our attachment to pleasure and our aversion to pain.

The *third* chakra, located in the solar plexus, brings vitality to the sympathetic nervous system. It is the center of will, personal power, self-control, and emotion. When it is awakened, we realize true freedom lies in mastering ourselves rather than controlling the outer world.

The *fourth* chakra, or the heart chakra, is located at the center of the chest. This chakra anchors the life force from the higher self[24] and energizes the body. It is the center of love and forgiveness and regulates our openness to life. When it is awakened, we move from conditional love ("I will love you, if you will love me") to the capacity for unconditional, divine love.

The *fifth* chakra, located at the throat, is the center for communication and finding one's voice as well as the center for physical, emotional, and mental purification. When this chakra is awakened, we begin the process of purification, realizing the impact that the toxicity of our thoughts, emotions, and bodies has upon us.[25]

The *sixth* chakra, or the third eye, vitalizes the lower brain and central nervous system and naturally regulates vision. When this chakra is activated, we gain wisdom, a deepening of our intuitive knowing,

---

24 Saraswati, The Chakras: Keys to Quantum Leap in Human Evolution.
25 Cohen, 1.

and the ability to see through the paradoxes of life. We listen to our internal guidance and *know* from personal experience or awareness rather than from what we have been told. At this level, we see the oneness of everything, which brings a level of sacred interaction into everyday life.

The *seventh* chakra, or the crown chakra, vitalizes the upper brain and rules, according to Neil S. Cohen, the "unification of the higher self with the human personality."[26] In contrast to the evolution through the first six chakras, the evolution of the seventh chakra has traditionally required the guidance and assistance of one who has succeeded in making this leap them self, such as a guru or enlightened teacher. The practice of Kriya yoga and other forms of yoga with the assistance of a live guru can set this transformative evolutionary process in motion. Divine grace plays a role in the activation of this chakra. The physical and nonphysical worlds become *one*.

Kriya yoga in particular hastens this process by opening the inner cerebrospinal pathway of ascension.[27] It is important to have a practitioner of the yoga sciences assisting this process, because premature movement of the powerful kundalini energy can be damaging, and the body must be prepared beforehand. In the same way that you wouldn't want to put a huge amount of electricity through too small a wire, the body must be capable of carrying the power of the kundalini. Paramahansa Yogananda explains that the kundalini arises along the spine, "releasing the soul through the spiritual eye into the kingdom of the Holy Ghost, the Christ Consciousness, and the Cosmic Consciousness of God the Father."[28]

In summary, it would seem that the Mayan calendar's energy of conscious co-creation, spiral dynamics' turquoise vMeme that is acting for the good of the whole, and the yoga sciences' union of the nonphysical and the physical are all aligned in their view of humanity's destiny. These different evolutionary models demonstrate that we are scheduled to be the Second Coming of Christ. So, in answer to

---

26   Ibid.
27   Yogananda, Paramahansa, "An AuthenticGlimpse of Jesus' Divine Life", 19.
28   Ibid, 19.

the question, "What is Christ consciousness?" I would say it's where a few individuals reside, where a few more tap occasionally, and hopefully where the rest are ultimately headed.

One more note of optimism: Ken Wilber, a leading philosopher and integral theorist, has said that there is a tipping point. When 5 to 10 percent of a population achieves a new structure of consciousness, that consciousness bleeds into the society and its structure initiating change. So we needn't be a full population in Christ consciousness to see its impact upon the world.

How can we make the most of this information? How would we act if we remembered the interconnectedness of all that we see? Imagine how differently we might respond, knowing that we are all that we see around us. And what if we were willing to make real life changes that reflected this knowledge?

Interconnectedness
Stop for a moment here and ask yourself, *Is there any place, activity, or state of mind in which I experience the interconnectedness of life? Where my heart opens and I feel gratitude?* For example, being in nature, meditating, or practicing yoga, tai chi, or chi gung may create this experience, as might exercising, surfing, skiing, swimming, serving others, caring for children, or doing the "seeing all as one" exercise.

Hiking often does this for me and makes me realize how taking care of myself is also part of being responsible for the whole.

Is there any part of me that would put the harmony of the earth over my own needs and wants? Or perhaps another way to look at this is to ask, *If everyone did what I do, what would the impact on the earth be?*

Most of this book is about our inward journey to assist our evolution and thus the world's; reaching outward to help the world has its place, too. There are many ways that I act from a place of being responsible for the world beyond my family and friends. This has included volunteering my time, giving to worthy causes, taking care of elderly neighbors, recycling, conserving water, keeping the thermostat down—these actions acknowledge that what I do matters and adds up, especially as we all do them. I have also meditated for world peace, to assist souls passing over during catastrophes, and to cap the oil leak in the Gulf of Mexico. The expansion of my world has expanded my capacity to help others.

It seems a bit mundane to end this chapter on the evolution to Christ consciousness talking about recycling! But it's a good metaphor. It wasn't all that long ago that recycling wasn't that common, and now most people do it. Manifesting Christ consciousness, seeing our interconnectedness, and taking a creator's responsibility for our world will soon be commonplace in the same way as recycling is now.

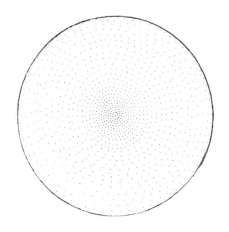

7. THE POWER TO MANIFEST

In the last two chapters, we defined Christ consciousness as "the Christed self indwelling and eternal as it exists in manifest expression through the living human form" and discovered our destiny as a species to embody it. Jesus surprised me as we continued our conversation:

Jesus: Yes, and much more is possible.

Hope: Like what?

Jesus: Well for example, bilocation, manifestation, and other demonstrations of the Christ condition.

The "Christed condition" Jesus mentions is documented extensively in *Life and Teaching of the Masters of the Far East* by Baird Spalding. The books refer to the masters' ability to bilocate (move from one location to another—even hundreds of miles away—almost instantly), walk on water, walk through fire, manifest food, and raise people from the dead. These are the same kinds of miracles that the Bible attributes to Jesus.

This may sound like the stuff of fairy tales, and yet these acts are possible. For example, Machaelle Small Wright manifests a cubic foot of manure and describes the process in detail in *Behaving as If the God in All Life Mattered.*[29] In *The Energy of Life*, one of the books about Anastasia, Vladimir Megre describes how he learned to teleport himself. He took his "second self" to spend three days in Cyprus, leaving his body lying on the couch at his home.[30] Having read about these amazing abilities in other "regular" people, my excitement built as I realized that these abilities really were what Jesus was describing when he described possible human expressions of Christ consciousness. I was eager to know more about how this was done, so I had the following conversation with Jesus:

Hope: Is it like Matthew 6:31–6:33? "So do not worry, saying, 'What shall we eat?' or 'What shall we drink?' or 'What shall we wear?' ... But seek first [your heavenly Father's] kingdom and his righteousness and all these things will be given to you as well"[31] (NIV).

Jesus: The quote perfectly describes the hierarchy of these energies. First *see* the kingdom of your heavenly Father, then *invite* it through your way of being on earth, and then, and only then, will the divine grace and the possibility of the perfect manifestation of all your needs come forth, through the right use of All That Is—which is within your power.

Hope: Can you say more on what it means to "rightly" use All That Is? Is this what is meant by "righteousness"?

Jesus: Right use is the offering of yourself as a divine vehicle and the knowing that all other beings and aspects of the physical world are in truth also divine vehicles. And so the way one is in the world is different when one knows this and acts from this place.

---

29 Wright, 138.
30 Megre, *The Energy of Life*, 193.
31 Scott, *The Greatest Words Ever Spoken*, 100.

Hope: So when one is seeing the kingdom and rightly using all that she sees, then the mighty divine power that is within and around her is available for manifestation?

Jesus: Yes, that is precisely it. The way through is to see all as yourself and then, of course, you have the potential of All That Is at your fingertips, so to speak …

It would seem that our needs will be met divinely when we *see* the world in a certain way—as the kingdom of God with perfect laws in action—and righteously (rightly use) all that we see.

In chapter four, we described the intention to embody Christ and then the act of doing so by treating all as ourselves. This is a third level of Christ expression: the "Christed condition."

Seeing Perfection

Before the fall from grace in the Bible story of Adam and Eve, humans lived on earth as gods, able to manifest all that they needed to sustain their physical bodies. Having one's needs met with ease was natural, and there was no premature death, disease, or suffering.

Paramahansa Yogananda, in his masterwork, *The Second Coming of Christ*, says that after the fall from grace, which Satan precipitated when he "manipulated the laws and principles of creation," "Satan turned the light of cosmic energy away from its focus on God and concentrated it on gross matter. The heaven-revealing astral light became the bedimmed physical luminaries of sun, fire, electricity, which show only material substances."[32] As this story is interpreted as a metaphor or as truth; in either case, it points to the path for revealing the Christ or the divine light that is within us. Looking inward is where we will discover the hidden divine light that lies there; it is no longer visible to the naked eye, but it is visible to our open hearts and our Christ eyes, where it is waiting to be acknowledged, revealed, and freed!

---

32 Yogananda, *The Second Coming of Christ,*142.

In *Life and Teaching of the Masters of the Far East*, Baird Spalding describes meeting and traveling with masters that at certain times were seen to emanate a soft light. They did not need a lamp as they walked indoors at night. The difference between us and masters or Christs is that they know of the divine light and have cultivated its presence so well that it is the *reality* of their lives and worlds. They are transparent to it and at present we are not.

On this topic, Jesus told me, "This means that the consciousness, the physical forms, and human growth and development have deteriorated to a degree that it is not possible to reclaim that perfected form without certain changes in consciousness.

"A person who sees *the system and process as perfect and unified* can patch it back together in a way that will reclaim, remount, and recreate it. What this means however is that the person must bolster the physical world himself. Like helping a wounded soldier to walk, the person holds the commitment to see only perfection in his sight. As an individual increases his access to this inner space of perfection, the ease with which the outer world may be perfect is also increased."

Manifestation becomes the natural result as we develop the capacity to see divine perfection in the system and process that creates everything around us. As we strengthen our ability to focus upon the divine process, and its unity or wholeness in all the seemingly separate and imperfect things our eyes take in, we are changing the world we live in, and thus the laws that rule our world. So the bolstering of the physical world that Jesus speaks of is our seeing divine perfection in the process that has created everything. As creators, our perception and view of the world defines the world we actually inhabit, so we can change the world and its laws, by changing our perception, seeing only the kingdom of God creates the kingdom of God. We become subject to laws that allow for instantaneous manifestation.[33]

---

33   In a communication that was cut from this document, Jesus offers A Punch List to Achieve Christ Consciousness, item number 4: *faith* speaks to this potential.
    Jesus: "Each one must come to the Christ Consciousness by his own path. There is only a general list of possible means. Each person is different."

That is a lot to take in! Being aware of the perfection all around us and looking inward can actually change the laws in action that rule the occurrences of our life. Our consciousness allows us to expand our divine creative potential into manifestation as we develop the capacity to embrace the perfect kingdom of God all around us.

In a conversation with one of the masters in *Life and Teaching of the Masters of the Far East*, one of Baird Spalding's party asked how the masters never became dirty or their clothing soiled—in contrast to him and his fellow journeyers. The master replied that it was more surprising to him that any of God's material could land where it wasn't meant to be. This illustrates a consciousness that sees perfection and doesn't know how to see otherwise!

Before you think, *I can't possibly do that*, read on, because you probably already are! There are levels of manifestation. Synchronicity, the miraculous and delightful alignment of needs with answers, is one level of manifestation. Although they don't

---

Hope: "What is that list?"

Jesus: "1st is the willingness, the desire, the vision/ experience of what this means. Without this, none of the others will manifest this state.
"2nd an offering- An offering of the self as vessel to receive the light of God in its fullest expression. Not only as a gift to the Earth and the Universe but as a demonstration of the love felt for this One Source.
"3rd harmony within the being. Body-Mind and Spirit aligned to the Truth: the understanding of the connectedness of all in conjunction with the willingness to take this knowing into application fully and completely.
"4th An unwavering faith that this is not only possible, but that 'this is so' and that all that is required is the faith that 'it is so' to 'make it so' (if it is not for some reason.)
"5th The understanding of life on the physical plane and what holds man in illusion. It means clarity on the difficulty of duality; the vice grip of good vs. bad and the endless nature of the illusion and its manifestations.
"6th and finally- the fairness and will to see the job through. The faint hearted may start, the bull headed may continue, but the one who finishes the job will gain the prize.
"These are the requirements that can bring a person to Christ self expression in complete manifestation of the light that is."

happen at our will and command, their frequency and reliability increases in our lives as seeing life as a perfect process becomes a practice. Life is sometimes filled with synchronicities: the amazing "coincidences" that defy all odds. No doubt you can think of some incidences in your own life when you manifested in this manner. For example, maybe you think of someone you haven't seen for *years,* and then you run into her at the grocery store that afternoon. Or as happened this morning, I was looking for the originals of the mandalas for this book, and couldn't find them anywhere. I had almost given up when I decided to straighten up my desk and found a photocopy of my son's passport which I wanted to put in a fireproof box, when I opened the box the mandalas were right there on top! (I had put them there for safekeeping and forgotten them...) A few years ago I was at a cabin in the woods, doing the illustrations for my last book, I was under a deadline and needed to find a photograph of a snake that was suitable to work from. I was flipping through a book with snake photographs, wishing I had one that was just right, when I heard a scream out on the porch. I ran outside to find the babysitter hopping around in horror as a tiny snake was struggling its way up through the porch boards! No doubt she thought I was crazy as I whooped with delight said "don't let it get away!" and ran to get a clear storage box with a top. I put it in the box, used it for the illustration, and let it go later that afternoon. Now what are the odds of that?

I realize that in those innocent desires and "thoughts to myself," there is great power and potential! I am thinking to "myself," but it's *myself* as the whole universe, and the universe has an infinite capacity to respond! Can you imagine the great computer in the sky kicking into action: beep, beep, snake being desired, coordinates 42.27 N by 72.94 W ...seeking nearest snake location ... checking, checking ... snake located ... creating impulse in snake to move to meet divine desire ...snake arrived ... request complete.

> **Synchronicities**
> Synchronicities occur all the time, just not always in the direction I would like! Two stories come to mind. I was unloading the dishwasher and thinking about my son breaking a cup the day before. In that same moment, I hit the handle of a mug against the edge of the counter, and it broke off. I kept the mug to remind myself of the perfect laws in action that create this perfect world! The other day, I was pouring water in my car from one water bottle to another. I wasn't holding it carefully and was afraid it would spill. It slipped out of my hand and drenched the car and me. I notice these occurrences and thank the perfect laws in action for reminding me of the power of my thoughts and fears. They leave me chagrined and reassured at the same time!

As one becomes more intentional in his manifesting, one can clearly visualize with thought, words, and emotion the end result wishing to be manifested.[34] In order to move to this level of manifestation one must understand the creative process, *know* it is possible, and have the focus to either hold his mind to it or let it go as appropriate.

> **Jesus**: What this means is that the perfection of the human reflects in the perfection of the world. The reflected world happily reveals that which the perfected human thinks upon. It is the actual joy of the world to create [fulfill the needs and desires] for this level of consciousness. Think of it this way: the earth is clay waiting to be molded into shape. The human, as she sees perfection, is able to mold the clay into the shapes that she imagines. It is really as simple as that. Thought, creation, form. But perfection at many levels is calling this and thus is making this possible." [The perfection of the human, and the perception the human uses, make manifestation possible.]

Our ability to create what we want demands a level of mastery over our bodies, our minds, our emotions, and the lens and depth through which we see the world.

---

34 Wright, *Behaving as If the God in All Things Mattered*, 141.

Hope: Is it true that mastery of our bodies gains us access to divine creative power?

Jesus: Not only is this so, but there is another issue that is worth mentioning here. The transcendence of the demands and infirmities of the human body will also offer you a clarity of focus that looking at the world through the filter of the body's needs cannot offer.

There is a fine line to draw here between appropriate response and slavish catering to our physical bodies and their demands. Jesus is pointing to a relationship with the body were one is first "All That Is" and second inhabiting a body with its needs. There are documented cases of people not needing food to survive for years at a time because they have learned to receive their sustenance directly from the sun and divine source energy.[35] Jesus isn't saying we must go that far, but he is pointing out that the body can limit our possibilities to manifest. Moving beyond the "infirmities of the human body system," as Jesus mentions, means transcending the body's view of the world by looking from a higher unified consciousness from which the body is just one aspect of our perspective. Our focus can then be upon the Divinity within everything instead.

The other night, I was in pain; my body hurt a lot. I had just been reading about looking inward to the Divinity's source or contact point for energy in a certain part of the brain. I was guided to sit in meditation and focus upon the medulla oblongata in the center of my head.[36] As I did this, the pain went away because I was focused on something much greater. The minute I lost my focus and returned to my body, the pain returned. This showed me how the filter of the body's pain changed how I saw the world. Being in pain is an extreme example, but whenever our bodies are cold, hungry, uncomfortable,

---

35 Yogananda, *The Second Coming of Christ*, 166. He references a book entitled *Amanzil* about Therese Neumann. The information was "taken from an address of Right Reverend Joseph Schrembs, D.D., Bishop of Cleveland." *Amanzil* was reprinted from the *The Catholic Universe Bulletin,*Clevland, OH (eleventh edition).

36 Ibid, 161.

or filled with artificial ingredients, refined sugars, and processed food, for example, these experiences and inputs put a filter on what we see in the world, and thus, they limit the possibility that we will see and know perfection.

We are upping the ante here—we are talking not only about walking on earth as the Christ but also of adding mastery or transcendence of the body *and* manifestation to the list! So what this clarifies for me, and hopefully for you, is that we are much more than we ever imagined, and when we live knowing that, we are capable of manifesting our every need. If we are to fulfill our divine mandate, our work is to walk the earth in Christ consciousness, seeing the perfect laws in action, treating everything as *one* and loving the creator of it all. When we are doing that, we are fulfilling our mission on earth.

Hope: Did I get that right, Jesus?

Jesus: Well, yes and no, for there is a subtlety that must be addressed. When one is seeing all as *one*, there is a way of doing so that *negates* oneself, and there is a way of doing so that *empowers* oneself. It is a key truth of the human journey that an individual's empowerment is the expression of divine energy incarnate.

The Role of Joy

Hope: How does joy relate to the expression of divine energy?

Jesus: Joy is the complete manifestation of the Christ energy in your expression of yourself, who you are, and what you came to offer. Joy is vibrant self-expression and the surety of knowing who and what you are.

As I see perfection around me, and see all as one, I observe the empowerment of my freer expression. There is more room for the Christ within me to move now. I move my body more lightly (I started dancing to the music when my cell phone rang the other day!), I spontaneously sing out loud more often, and I no longer allow limiting thoughts to always have the *last* word in my internal dialogues. I realize that I am empowering the part of myself that is spontaneous and joyful.

The Role of Love
Seeing perfection is closely tied to love. In the Bible (Luke 10:27), Jesus Christ said, "Thou shalt love the Lord thy God with all thy heart, and with all thy soul, and with all thy mind, and with all thy strength; and thy neighbor as thyself" (KJV).

Hope: Please explain the quote and the role of love.

Jesus: Always there are ways to get somewhere on earth—this way or that way, easy or hard, shorter or longer. What this describes is a linear physical world. If one wishes to transform *one's own* world and transcend its limitations, one must seek a higher set of laws for examination. For example, the quote you ask about: "Thou shalt love the Lord thy God with all thy heart, and with all thy soul, and with all thy mind, and with all thy strength; and thy neighbor as thyself." What this offers is the literal energetic road to a transformed world that transcends limitation. Now, why is this? It is possible because of the way the physical and nonphysical worlds interface. They penetrate each other fully and deeply. So, in affecting or manipulating the physical world [which includes the world of thought], one gains access through resonance[37] to the worlds beyond it. To truly embrace and apply these words is the bridge to the beyond, that gateway to your freedom and the hope of humanity.

Hope: How is it that the love of the Source does all that?

---

37 Resonance is communication of things of like vibration, so in thinking a certain way, connection is made to the non physical worlds through harmonic resonance, and those human thoughts thus penetrate and affect the non physical world.

Jesus: When one loves the Source as oneself, one is in alignment with the truth of "All that Is." For there is only "self." There is only love, and in that union, one aligns with the power of All That Is. From that place of alignment, the flow of energy from the highest levels is possible, and thus there is a new potential that exists on earth. For this to occur, the person must truly be in a space of complete and unconditional love with All That Is and in a space of complete surrender and release of oneself as an individual entity on earth. Now, it is not possible to completely release the self, or the being would cease to exist, but the degree to which one is in surrender is the degree to which one is in alignment with truth and the degree to which one's works on earth may reflect the true glory and potential of the divine self in expression on earth. This is the true glory of God.

So here Jesus tells us how we may become the Christ: "Love the One, the true, the Divinity in all that you see." When you look at something that does not appear to be divine perfection, you needn't try to convince yourself that it is. You simply look within its outer form and see the Divinity that is within it, the creative process that birthed it, and thus the innate divine perfection within its form.[38]

An Exercise for Perceiving Perfection

There is an energetic framework that exists within physical things. The energy exists like a three dimensional blueprint within the physical form. They define the same thing, just at different levels of demonstration. The physical world *is a result* of the energetic world that creates it. How is the energetic world created? It is kind of like God created a computer program created long ago, and humans are empowered with the code that allows them to create. The problem is that humans don't realize they are programming as they go through life and are creating rogue programs! Perhaps when we see perfection in everything and love unconditionally, that's like having God's password enabling us to create a more pleasing world! So step back one giant step,

---

38 Spalding, *Life and Teaching of the Masters of the Far East*, vol. 4, 154.

and look at the physical world with the understanding that it is a *perfect reflection of the energetic world within it*. If you can do this, it will help you to accept the world as it is and empower you to create (with thoughts and emotions) the energetic template of a changed world.

An exercise for perceiving perfection: stop for a moment and see the underlying perfection that lies within this book or something in front of you. The universal laws that created it are perfect; it is the perfect result of the underlying creative energy, vision, and physical materials that it is made of. Say, for example, that it is something that is not perfect in its performance or in its current state (it is broken or dirty); it is nonetheless perfect because of the universal process that formed it, its molecular structure, and its function at a deep level within it. It remains perfect even while broken because the cause of its imperfection is also following perfect universal laws! So the perfection that the masters see and know is the deep level of perfection inherent in the process of creation itself.

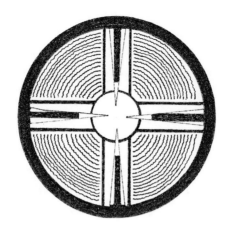

8. WHY CHRIST CONSCIOUSNESS?

If the ability to manifest isn't enough, there are several more reasons to seek Christ consciousness.

Creativity

Animals, plants and other living beings are not able to create as we do. They have prescribed roles in the natural world from which they are unable to deviate. An apple tree cannot choose to create other than apples. A deer is a deer made by the Source; it has no ability to deviate from that template. In contrast, humans have a role as creators on earth. Our free will gives us the right and responsibility to create as we please without divine dictates determining what we create. It is entirely up to us. Jesus speaks of this when he says,

> How can God-energy get into expression except through man? There is not another organism upon the whole Earth that can vibrate at the same rate or frequency; and in consequence, it is so highly organized that it does perceive, then generate and transform this supreme energy, which enables man to express God to the whole world. How can this be done except through

the highly organized and perfected body which is when you are in full control of that body?[39]

In August of 1998, I got a channeled reading from Martha, who later became a good friend. In preparation for the reading, she asked if I had questions for my spirit guides. Aside from my questions, she suggested I ask, "What is my greatest gift?" I was on a road trip with my husband when I received the channel. The guides told her that I was an artist and that I was psychic, among other things. This was news to me! I was so eager to try out being an artist that I couldn't wait to get home. We stopped at an art supply store in some small town in Maine that same day and bought a pad and some colored pencils. I put the bag of art supplies on my lap. For the entire day, I would place the bag on the dashboard as I got out of the car, and upon my return, I would put the bag back on my lap. It was almost as though I had found a part of my creative self and was not willing to let my connection to it out of my sight.

In the weeks afterward, I started to draw and then later, to paint, and I discovered I loved it. As I got ideas for painting that had some expressive message in them, I became energized and needed less sleep in a way I had never experienced before. Creativity came roaring up through me, as my love for the earth found expression through paint. These paintings are of a different quality than ones I did of commonplace subjects that had just caught my eye. I realize in retrospect that this energy was the creative arm of the Christ within.

Heightened creativity and energy are also a result of Christ consciousness. Engagement with the world, in whatever field you are inspired to express yourself in, takes the creative expression of the Christ within outward into manifestation. Divine inspiration is both a personal and commonplace expression of what fills *you* with joy, and it is the cutting edge of consciousness experiencing and evolving through us.

---

39 Spalding, *Life and Teaching of the Masters of the Far East*, vol. 3, 49.

Divine Inspiration

Stop here a moment and think about the people that you admire whose creations and lives have expanded the world in some way. Perhaps they were divinely inspired to create or live as they did. People like Ludwig van Beethoven, Winston Churchill, Leonardo da Vinci, Amelia Earhart, Saint Joan of Arc, Helen Keller, Claude Monet, Maria Montessori, Georgia O'Keeffe, Sacagawea, William Shakespeare, Harriet Beecher Stowe, and Mother Theresa surely were. Where in your life do you express divine inspiration? What brings you joy?

Happiness

Regardless of our circumstances, the gift of a body here on the earth at this pivotal moment in time is a treasure. If the universe has a lottery, you have won it, because it is from within a body that we have experiences that help us to evolve our consciousness. Through our lives' experiences, we become *motivated* to evolve. A more highly evolved person suffers less and has more choices in how to respond to life.

Think of when you have felt anxious, frustrated, or angry, and think of the choices you were able to make in that moment. Most likely, they were reactive and limited. Then think of a time when you were feeling joyful, loving, or accepting and recall the choices open to you at that time. If you practice this awareness, you will see that the higher emotions consistently offer you more choices in the range of responses you are capable of.[40] Your life is happier when you have Christ consciousness not necessarily because your outer circumstances have improved but because of the change in your perspective and attitude.

The Opportunity to Transcend Reincarnation

We all elected to be in bodies here on earth because we are awakening to knowing ourselves as all being one and thus freeing our Christ

---

40 Hawkins, *Transcending the Levels of Consciousness: The Stairway to Enlightenment*, 32.

selves from their prisons within our previously unconscious human forms! So, the answer to "Why Christ consciousness?" is that our souls have *already* chosen it and have been working toward it for many, many lifetimes, trying to get to this one! Our awakened consciousness is the engine that allows us to evolve at speeds much faster than would be otherwise possible. Without awakened consciousness we create karma, which like cement shoes, holds us in the cycle of reincarnation for lifetimes. Both our personal karma and humanity's collective karma hold us captive to reincarnation. In Christ consciousness, we don't create additional karma.

I received this channel in 2010:

The transcendence of reincarnation is a possibility when the One Source is the only reference for an individual. No longer must one choose to see life as imperfect and oneself, too, as imperfect. There can be a transcendence of incarnation through the unification of self with All That Is. All that one must take from this is an understanding that as one applies and lives the One Truth, this reincarnation will no longer have its magnetic hold on you.

The transition to the nonphysical world, or death, is a timeless and space-less passage. It only offers the one moment; there is no past or future, because there is no physical form. So it would be logical that being in Christ consciousness at the moment of death would offer a baseline from which our next lifetime might be vibrationally built. This makes sense in a world where the vibration (consciousness) we have in any moment is the point from which we are creating. The fact that *yesterday* we were in Christ consciousness may not help us if we die today! Not knowing when (or if)[41] we might be whisked from

41 I say "or if" here, leaving the possibility of never leaving the body as a potential. There are references to people living for many hundreds of years in the Bible, and in a pre-fall from grace world, death was *elected* after the completion of the lifetime, not *required* after an arbitrary number of years on earth that in the collective consciousness described "a lifetime." In addition scientists say that no cell in our body is older than 7 years, so wouldn't it make sense that the body is meant to be kept indefinitely, until it no longer serves the spiritual journey for which it was created?

our bodies, why not start being *unified* with All That Is right now? A next lifetime insurance policy!

Self Compassion

Self-compassion is key. I often think of this when I have lost myself in a reactive tirade. I awake to the present moment, clean up my energetic offering, and my human nature wants to criticize myself for my reaction. But that is a trap that has caught me too often. I try to remember that the only thing that matters is *how I am right now* because this *now* is creating the future. Surprisingly, self-compassion is the bridge to the future world, where I can be less reactive. If I chastise myself, I return to the past and just send myself around the same loop again, whereas if I see through the eyes of Christ and realize reactivity is a human pattern that we all struggle with, not mine alone, I can find compassion for myself, *make amends to anyone I harmed*, and move on.

Christ Consciousness Is What We Are *Already* Searching For

A physical lifetime is a constant search for something that will satisfy us in a deep and lasting way. We aspire to job, financial, relationship, and lifestyle goals in the expectation that they will "make us happy"—for good. Until we are conscious of our union with the One, which is and *always* has been, we will continue to search in all the wrong places for what we mistakenly think will make us happy.

Reunion with our divine selves, the embodiment of the Christ within us, is the only thing that can make us truly happy. Divinity is hiding within us and in everything around us. All we need to find it is to know it is there and act from that knowledge. Divinity is a master of disguise. So how do we find it? When we act *as if* it is there, it appears! When you act as though everything around you is divine, Divinity reveals itself to you.

> **Seeing the Sacred**
>
> I was hurriedly opening a bag of frozen peas on Christmas Day, 2010. The bag burst open, and peas flew everywhere. I knew I had been rushing and felt grateful for the reminder to slow down, come back into the moment. I put the bag down, lowered myself to my knees, and started picking up the peas. I picked them up one at a time, with each hand, seeing them and the act of gathering them as sacred. It isn't necessarily the grand acts that bring the Christ into form; it's the little ones, too. When we do things in a sacred manner, as though touching the Divinity, the results of those actions carry that same sacred energy. That's why food cooked with love tastes better. (I don't remember whether the divine peas got rinsed and put into the pot.)
>
> Stop reading for a moment and imagine that something or someone nearby is divine, or sacred and precious. As you make this shift in perspective, what changes do you observe in your body? How do you feel? What do you know about the thing you are seeing as sacred?

The Mantle

I bet you didn't know there was a uniform for Christ consciousness, too; it's invisible!

man·tle: noun. 1. a loose, sleeveless coat worn over outer garments. 2. Anything that covers, envelops, or conceals.[42]

> **Jesus**: The mantle of Christ is what one energetically wears in the consciousness of the Christ self. Unseen, but not unfelt, the mantle holds a powerful gentility, a focused compassion, a loving demeanor. Not only is this mantle a true and tangible (energetic) thing, but also it is a gift for those who come near it. Not only is there an emanation of the Christed source energy from this mantle, but also there is a gift of lifting upward for

---

42 *American Heritage Dictionary of the English Language*, 1st ed., s.v. "mantle."

those who pass nearby. What this means, in effect, is a rising of energy in those who are in proximity to this energy.

The real issues that occur for one in this consciousness are clarity, oneness with all,[43] the inhabiting of the present moment, and the expression of one great organism of life— that one is a tiny fractal perspective of life and everything around one is the rest. The one organism is not only made up of humans but also trees and rocks and plants and animals and the energies that hold them and are behind them.

One can't really claim the mantle. The process of embodying the Christ consciousness is not like an acquisition (which is hard to understand—I speak from experience!). It is the opposite. One does not acquire it; one strips and becomes empty to uncover it, discover it, and set it free. One surrenders to allow it to manifest. One sinks down into him or her self so deeply that the outer shell hiding the deepest self collapses through lack of feeding and support.

Baird Spalding explains this quite clearly when he says, "The trouble with the masses of humanity today is that they are trying to become something that is already right within. We are seeking and searching everywhere outside of ourselves for God, attending countless lectures, meetings, groups; reading innumerable books; looking to teachers and personalities and leaders; when all the time God is right within. If mankind will let go of the *trying* and accept that they *are,* they will soon be perfectly aware of the reality."[44]

In summary, the reasons to choose Christ consciousness are heightened personal creativity, the chance to assist God-energy to get into expression, greater happiness, and more choices. Christ consciousness also brings the opportunity to transcend the cycle of reincarnation when we finally identify ourselves as the One Source. We also find the deep satisfaction of having discovered what we are

43 " Oneness with all", means defining oneself as that greater being, and the "expression of one great organism of life" illustrates the action of the person as coming form that greater definition of self.

44 Spalding, *Life and Teaching of the Masters of the Far East*, vol. 5, 99.

truly looking for and, last but not least, the mantle, our energetic "gift for those who come near it," as Jesus said.

The next stop on our journey is the discovery of how we travel from human consciousness to Christ consciousness.

9. SURRENDER

Surrender is a state of non-judgment about what is. What the universe offers up in each and every moment is perfect. To see that is a wonderful thing. When one sees from this perspective, there is a clarity that follows, a wisdom that flows, and a serenity that emanates.

—a favorite quote from my guidance

As I was writing this chapter I had a dream: While walking hip-deep in the water on the beach, a wave swept me off my feet. Realizing I had my bathing suit on, I didn't *resist* and floated happily along, letting the water sweep me down to where I cheerily chatted with some ladies on the beach. Then another swift current swept me along, and I philosophically went with it, not fighting it or trying to change anything about my situation.

My dream illustrates what surrender is like. We surrender to what is happening in this moment, *now*. We release the past and the future, and clarity, wisdom, and serenity result. When the Christ consciousness enters your life, it is like this. You are still your personality, but the water, the wave, or the ocean itself is really in charge as the greater you.

Jesus clarifies what *surrender* means:

> **Jesus**: What often occurs is that surrender sounds like, well, surrender—"lift the white flag, we have failed"—when in truth, surrender is ease and true attainment of living "what is," here and now, in alignment with what has been created through law. This is surrender. This is the place from which all things are possible.
>
> The opposite of surrender is resistance. In resistance to what is, we have lots of friction that we stir up in our lives, making things much harder and draining our energy. So, in surrender we have attained—we have succeeded in living the truth of—what is. This doesn't mean we won't seek to change what is; it simply means that we accept that this is what is right here and now. And this is the platform from which we will move into the next moment of our reality.
>
> **Hope**: Is surrender of the small self required to allow the expression of the higher self through?
>
> **Jesus**: What is required is surrender, yes, but not surrender to … the ego-based human body system. No longer does one robotically respond to the ego. One is taking orders from the higher level. It is a shift in who is boss but not necessarily a complete surrender of all expression of the human personality. One needn't worry about disappearing. One will only become a grander, more stable, more brilliant version of who one already is. For the connection to the One Source will be stronger and more potent, so there will be less of a barrier to accessing this part of oneself.

The Ego
I define the ego here as any part of myself that holds me from my true nature.

> **Hope**: Jesus, where does ego fit in?

Jesus: Dear one, ego holds us from our true nature, so when we *see* this force clearly in our lives, we are empowered to step beyond it. We don't only step beyond it in the outward expression of our lives but also in the constant inner turmoil the ego can create. The ego *thrives* on separation for breakfast, lunch, and dinner! So, in seeing all as *one*, we essentially transform the world we see and make it *uninhabitable* to the ego! The ego then starves and ultimately loses its power to control us in negative ways. The ego may be useful at times to keep us surviving as individual human bodies, and that is its simple and healthy function—not as the master of our actions!

Hope: So, in the new world we create of seeing *one*, we go where the ego can't follow us?

Jesus: Yes, precisely. Not only that, the ego is left behind to wither away so that all the energies it previously commandeered to maintain itself are redirected to the more functional use of Christ expression through the human form.

Hope: So, I *do* need to see the ego to understand its ways and attitudes in order not to be tempted back into seeing separation over and over?

Jesus: Yes, and the knowing of the self is easiest from seeing all as *one*. It's like this. The ego is camouflaged as your self: your likes and dislikes, behaviors, judgments, and ideas about how life is. These are ego's trappings. If you then shine the light of oneness upon life, *then* things become clear. You can *see* what part is ego and become clear of its control simply by seeing all as one. So the practice of seeing all as one both maintains your presence in a new world *and* renders evident the ego, which was previously camouflaged so well. This is what is meant by "know thyself," something rendered possible through the perspective of truth or oneness. That is all. Namaste. We are One!

In seeing all as one, we put our egos on notice … maybe even give them the pink slip!

There is no need to feel embarrassed for all the clever things your ego has done to help you be more _____(fill in the blank)_____ than everyone else. We all do it! It is simply the way of the ego, and it has served its purpose. We can disarm it when we name it, admit it, and speak about its presence in our actions as they occur.

When I first did this, I found myself having "ego backlash"—being more impatient, angry, and frustrated than ever! Don't be surprised or think that you are making no progress; it's actually a good sign, because the backlash indicates that the ego is feeling threatened! It makes the ego easier to see, too.

One excellent tool for disarming the ego is to align with a higher purpose that motivates your actions and direction in life.[45] When I sense the ego's presence, I realign with the surrendered self, the part of me that remains loving, open, humble, and with a higher purpose. Now, with a conscious act of will to realign with a higher purpose, sometimes I can free myself.

Recognizing Ego
Stop for a moment and think about how ego is present in your life. When/where do you see it most strongly? Why do you suppose that is?

Dark vs. Light
The dark side of me exists. The light side of me exists. That's the yin and yang of life. Why do I wish I could just become light? Acceptance and self-compassion for this condition in me and in others is my bridge to wholeness. When I shrink from my dark side, I fragment myself. But when I realize that this is just the human condition and say, "Hey, dark and light make up the whole," the meaning I make from darkness's presence is completely different. My dark side loses its power over me. And then, too, my attachment to the light lessens … and voilà, I am united.

---

45 Hamilton, *The Evolutionary Life Transformation Program.*

Conscious Attention

Conscious attention allows the Christ within to be expressed, as opposed to acting and reacting unconsciously. I sometimes think of conscious attention as cultivating "the observer" in my life.

> **Hope**: What does conscious attention do?

> **Jesus**: Conscious attention allows the human individual that has chosen a path toward God expression to allow that expression to manifest through the individual's body.

So, conscious attention is necessary to manifest Christ consciousness.

> **Hope**: I am confused. How do surrender ... and conscious attention harmonize?

> **Jesus**: Dear one, the relationship between surrender and conscious attention is simple. The first, surrender, allows the other to occur. Once one is surrendered, the state of that person's mind is in a neutral or receptive position. From this place, she has the ability to move energy and information from her higher self to her body-mind complex.[46] And, thus, the possibility of conscious attention is made ready.

Surrendering to our divine internal guidance and to what this present moment holds makes conscious attention possible, and we become, as Jesus said before, "more stable, more brilliant version[s] of who [we] already [are]."

---

46 Humans have energetic bodies in addition to the visible physical body. The "body-mind complex" Jesus speaks of here, refers to the other energy bodies in conjunction with the physical body.

Jesus's Invitation to Christ Consciousness

Here Jesus offers the invitation for us to make a commitment to Christ consciousness.

Jesus: We are one in our thoughts, words, and deeds when we have attuned our hearts to the one truth of who we are. It is only when our attunement wavers that we find suffering, separation, and dissolution of the human body.

Wandering the halls of earth aimlessly, most people find little to be joyful for since their thoughts, words, and deeds are centered around and created from an energy that is a faulty impostor of truth. In many disguises, this imposter tempts the unwary, offering baubles and beads when true gold is desired. Unsuspecting humans are mesmerized by their ancestors' mistakes into thinking that life is hard work and suffering, when there is nothing further from the truth.

What must come from this and other sources of the divine is a road map to the place beyond the mirage that earth has become. Not only is there timeless wisdom ready and wanting to share, but also the places at the table have been set, dear reader, awaiting *your* arrival. Cast off your glasses that hold you apart, lay down your burdens that seem so many, and lift your sights to love: to loving the One, the True, the Divinity in all that you see. And thus, you will become all of this too.

I am your savior only in that I have shown the way so that you, too, may join the list and ranks of those who are truly free.

Signed: *Jesus Christ* _____ Christ
(your name here)

I remember the many internal debates I had on the journey of surrender to a higher power. I had been trained to believe that the minute you surrendered to God, your life was no longer your own. I had no idea what I was surrendering to and I didn't want to be surrendering in some Roger Milktoast kind of way. What is it that kept me from surrender? I had no idea at the time, but I can now see that it was the cost of the parts of my life that couldn't accept my unity with All That Is and the decisions that that perspective might have required. As you decide for yourself what the investment might be, depending on how far you are from unity consciousness, you will find that it may be a pittance or a king's ransom! It is well worth it either way. In seeing through the eyes of One, the world is completely and instantaneously *transformed*.

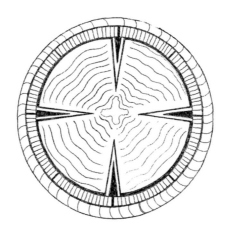

10. HOW TO COMMUNICATE WITH YOUR INNER CHRIST

Well, if I am not following the ego's demands anymore, and I am willing to surrender to the Christ within, how will I know what my Christ self wants? The guides offer this: "Begin now by sitting still; hold your focus upon your breath. Notice all the parts of your physical being that would steal your focus away. Pay them no mind and return to your breath. If you do this often enough, you will find a greater peace comes over your being, which will facilitate your receptivity to communication with the divine being that is the greater aspect of yourself."

Our inner guidance is tailored specifically for us. We often look outside ourselves for guidance, which serves no purpose if we truly understand what we have access to *within* ourselves. It's like having a personal radar system that can see from an expanded perspective and bring you information you wouldn't have otherwise. It also ultimately brings you faith in the process of life, with less focus on the outcome.

Meditate

Stillness in your outer and inner worlds opens your receptivity and helps your inner divine self. Being completely still each day for even a few minutes creates a space for your inner guidance to break through the static that modern life puts in our minds and bodies. Regularly sitting in meditation is a good way to achieve and maintain this stillness. When you are through, ask, "Is there anything I need to know now?" It might bring you helpful guidance. An alternative to meditating is to engage in something that takes just a little bit of focus but not too much, such as sweeping, raking, or other simple work. Many times when I have had a question, the answer has popped into my head as I was doing something unrelated to it.

I ask Jesus if there is a difference between our inner Christ selves and the guidance that comes through our bodies' "gut feelings":

> **Jesus**: The guidance that comes to you is always appropriate if it comes while you are in a state of calm. What causes the opening for detrimental or disharmonious energies to gain entry is the vibration one offers from a place of imbalance or disharmony. When we are out of balance, we attract this condition. What is required is a calm centering so you attract the same. So go ahead and act on your gut feeling as it comes to you. Act on your communicated words when they are clear and calm and feel right to you.

> **Hope**: I have been using "inner self" and "Christ self" interchangeably, and I just had the thought, *what if they are different?*

> **Jesus**: As in all things, everything is relative and vibrational. The inner aspect of the self can be the Christ self, or it can be a lesser version of the Christ self; one takes the level that one is able to access in the moment.

> There is no rule that says that everything you access is the Christ self or that the information will be helpful in the moment.

Not only must you run a quality control assessment on the information conveyed through your words and emotions and thoughts, but also you must always decide through your own filters what the appropriate guidance is. Never fully accept the words at face value, and always examine them in the face of what you see and feel on earth. Namaste. We are *one*.

Jesus is saying that discernment is an ongoing practice as one learns to navigate the internal relationships with one's many egoic selves, the Christ self, and the guides.

Learn the Language
The truth is that we are all *one*, and we cannot separate ourselves even if we try. Therefore, in creating a dialogue with our inner guidance, we need to be sure that we don't forget our wholeness. The language that the One speaks is not just words. Intuition is one way to describe its internal language.

Making room for intuition and acting upon it can strengthen it. Phrases like "I have an inkling," "an impulse," "a gut feeling," or "I just know" describe an internal communication; when you find yourself saying or thinking these phrases, follow the impulse and see what happens. In observing the results of your follow-through, you will learn to know and trust this inner guidance. Formal written communication is channeling, also known as automatic writing. That is another way to access your intuition that makes use of your physical body.

The One is also communicating with us through our environments. Sometimes when I am rushing and driving too fast, birds will swoop across my windshield to slow me down. I have intended not to move through my days at a rush; therefore I give permission to the universe for this kind of support when I start to rush! Messages come in many ways: feathers falling from the sky remind me of the magic and mystery I am immersed in, swooping butterflies remind me to stop and appreciate the beauty of life, and a gust of wind incites me to movement or a change in direction. An acorn on the head is a serious call to wake up. Then there are songs on the radio with lyrics that say just what is going on right now for me, or numbers on the clock like 11:11 and 12:12, which affirm that my energy is in alignment with the guides. Books literally fall off the shelf or draw my attention when I need to read them, and friends are often messengers with wise perspectives. The sunlight shining through a forest of ice-covered twigs is so breathtaking that it makes me cry and opens my heart to life. A person who jostles me reminds me to be gentler, and when nothing goes right, I stop to recheck the decisions I have made. When a luscious, warm brownie that is halfway to my mouth falls on the floor, I know it won't make me feel good and that I shouldn't eat it. There are infinite ways that we communicate with the One, and as we open to this awareness, the world talks to us like a good friend, guiding, encouraging, correcting, and walking along beside us. When this happens, life is magical!

Discerning Ego's Resistance to the Spirit's Guidance

Recently, I debated for weeks whether to go to a conference in Sedona, Arizona. I would feel excitement about it and then immediately feel like it was too much, that I shouldn't go. This went on until I bought the airline tickets and signed up for the conference, feeling like I would *never know why* I was so confused unless I went. I felt a nervous contraction in my belly after I bought the tickets. The night before the trip, I felt so sick that I thought I needed to go to the emergency room (I wanted to cancel the trip). As I got in the car to go to the hospital, my guides said "Just lie on the grass," which I did instead. I felt better after clicking into nature's healing vibration and commanding my cells to return to their divine perfection. When I remembered a phrase that Mary the healer had told me to say, "Oh yeah, this is just illusion," I got up perfectly fine! The next morning, when I was due to leave for the airport, I hoped my ride wouldn't show up—but he did.

On the way to the airport, I started feeling panic, which built until I was in the security line and my former husband called me. He reassured me that he sensed it was fine. I was in a cold sweat, with pressure in my lungs and throat. I did get on the plane, thinking, *If this plane crashes, I am the stupidest person on earth!* I Arrived in Phoenix safely, met my friend Michael, who had also flown in, rented a car, and drove to Sedona carefully … waiting for something to happen. I had no idea what.

On the second night, it happened. We were in a vegan restaurant that had a room filled with rocks and crystals. There were several huge Shiva Lingams, one even standing five feet tall. I had the impulse to sit on—or more correctly was *directed to* sit on—a Shiva Lingam that was lying sideways on the floor against a tree.

Shiva Linghams are shaped like elongated eggs. They are made of cryptocrystalline quartz mined from the bottom of the Narmada River in India. Twice I resisted my guidance's direction to sit on the rock, as I felt awkward about sitting on the display. Finally, at the third impulse, I grudgingly said internally, *Oh, Okay!"* wondering why the guidance was so insistent.

When I did sit on the Lingham, I felt a strong tingling in my neck and head. The counterclockwise motion, which Michael measured with his pendulum, was the energy quality of movement toward spirit. (Something we both learned while studying Biogeometry. (The clockwise motion is the movement towards physical life.)) Unaware, I relaxed and leaned back against the tree. My mind separated from my body, or perhaps it became so still that it seemed to disappear. My mind would return occasionally, but it felt inconsequential, mosquito-like. When it did succeed in getting my attention and urged me to get up (it had been an hour!), something was different.

I didn't wish to talk or move. When my mind convinced me that I had to get up, I just stood there. I couldn't walk. I finally moved when I again remembered Mary's phrase, "Oh yeah, this is all just illusion," and with that, I walked out to the car, kind of sloshing around in my body. I was *still* internally, and I moved my body minimally, methodically, like I was in a heavy costume!

I think the experience was an energetic version of diarrhea and vomiting: a good clean out! It took me twenty-four hours to return to somewhat normal. But I was not the same. Afterward I was less needy on the human level, more relaxed, and steady. I can see now why my ego had put up such resistance to the trip; it feared on some level that it would lose its control of my mind—something I had asked for and had been unable to achieve on my own.

Having studied the relationship with my guidance, I was confused by the experience and unsure just what had happened on the Lingam. Was it "good or bad"? I was reassured when my friend Les, who was living in the Middle East, called to say he'd had a vision of me spinning counterclockwise really fast, and that he was told to tell me that things were taken out of me and nothing was put into me. That was a relief!

I looked in *The Book of Stones* by Robert Simmons and Naisha Ahsian and found this description, which sounds quite accurate: "Shiva Lingams are emblems of inner transformation, partaking of the Storm element in order to break up patterns of self-limiting habits and beliefs, so one may be flooded with Spirit. Like Shiva, they destroy what is old and corrupt to clear the way for rebirth. Those who wish for such transformation will find in them a fierce and ready ally."[47] I had been asking for help in moving beyond my old, worn out, reactive patterns, and this gave my guidance permission to lead me to just the right situation to achieve that clean out!

How to Channel

First begin by seeing all as one, as Jesus teaches. From this place of unity with All That Is, we are in the best space to open a dialogue

47 Simmons and Ahsian, *The Book of Stones*, 360.

with our guides. This is how Martha taught me: with a pen and paper in hand, ask out loud or silently, "Is there anything I need to know right now?" Write down what comes to you immediately. It will feel like it is "you," and it is you, but it is also your guides speaking. If you do this regularly, you may find over time that more information flows to you after you ask this question. Suspend your disbelief, and just *write it down*!

Whatever comes quickly before you can think or evaluate it, write it down. You may be surprised to find that the information is useful and coherent and comes with more fluidity and detail as you practice. Sometimes when the words come, they sound like things you already know. I find, however, that upon rereading, they are always able to offer a new perspective.

When I first channeled, I got a single word, then a sentence, and later a paragraph, until finally one day a full page of writing ended with, "Ask me a question." What a delightful shock that was. It was like a stranger miraculously appeared out of nowhere. I, of course, said, "Who *are* you?" That was when Shadrach and I began our conversations. Knowing that I am never alone is an amazing way to live.

Intend to speak only to your higher self, your guides, and the greater part of you that exists in nonphysical form. "Like attracts like" is one of the vibrational laws of creation, and if you are calm and centered, you will attract the same kind of guidance. Communication will be positive or *solution*-based. The perspective of one who sees beyond the illusion of earth is the big picture perspective that comes from a place of unconditional love. These impulses can powerfully assist one's navigation through life.

A friend was told in January that she would move in November, but it was the November a year later that she ended up moving! Time on the higher levels is not the same as time here on earth. Look to include the signs you receive along the way to accomplish your guidance.

Act from Stillness

My guidance explained, "It is really a game of 'sit, be still, act as guided'; then move from the place of stillness into action. Action would have you at its beck and call, and what you must see is that *stillness* must have you at its beck and call. Stillness is your true master, and from stillness must all action originate. Namaste. We are one."

If it sounds right, do what is asked of you, and then observe the results. As you respond, you will become clear about their authenticity and whether you are hearing clearly. The merit of some actions can't be known right away, but if you stay aware of the process and *continue* to question your clarity and your connection, you will remain empowered and open to learning. But *do act*. If you don't take action, you are simply cluttering your mind with more information and devaluing the guidance. Practicing what they offer you gives you the full benefit of your communication and helps you to be confident in your guidance. Finally, don't forget to thank them— imagine how frustrating it must be to watch us all on earth!

I asked about channeling's role: "Dear one, channeling is a gift when it is used appropriately. 'Appropriate use' means that you use it to uplift and harmonize your life. It is an offering from the heavens to get you pointed in the right direction with the right shoes on your feet for the road ahead. It is a road map or sign for the time ahead … It will not tell you all the future; it will help you to put life in perspective from where you are *now*."

Sometimes guidance will direct me spontaneously, or I will ask for help. For example, there are times when they ask me to do something, or to go somewhere, and I have no real understanding of why. Sometimes I am pleasantly surprised by what occurs when I follow the impulse that they create within me. I may run into someone I haven't seen for a long time or it may be that I am needed in service. I remember a spring day in New York City: I was walking up Madison Avenue when the guides said, "Give that man some money." Now the man was walking along pretty fast, he was well dressed, and he was *not* begging. I thought, *How am I going to do that without embarrassing him (or myself)?* Well it "came to me" to run up from behind him and say to him, "Excuse me, sir, but you dropped this" while handing him some money. So I got the money out and did just that. To my great relief, he took it without blinking an eye, without any surprise, and continued walking! I feel like a secret agent when things like that happen.

Another time, on a Saturday morning the October after I had moved to my new home in the country, my son was with me, and we needed something to do that was fun for an eight-year-old. Guides had us get in the car and directed me: go left, right, straight, left, etc. We ended up in a town fifteen minutes away that I had never been to and pulled up at a harvest fair. It had hayrides, a field filled with pumpkins, a magic show, hot dogs for sale, and swarms of other kids to play with. That day was a delight all around. It takes faith to be led in that way, but more often than not, it has meaningful results. It makes for a life that is definitely not dull! I notice a drop in my energy when I don't follow through, as if I have disappointed my self … and I'll never know what I missed.

Intention

In this world, where all things have an opposite, "good" and "bad" can be interchangeable relative to one's perspective. For example, is it good or bad to drill a well to serve a village that had no well before? You might be tempted to say "good." But what about when the well ultimately lowers the water table, killing vegetation, causing the desert to expand, and displacing families and villages? Then would you change your assessment? "Good" and "bad" can be relative depending on the lens through which you see the results of your actions.

The intention to act for the highest good can assist you to find your way through earth's duality and can actually create your desired outcome. The very same "neutral" act can have entirely different consequences depending upon your intention. Your role is to be clear in your intention. Be clear about what you desire, visualize it, feel the emotions that it would bring to you and others. Sometimes I say, "If it be for the highest and best good" as a preamble—just to cover myself. That old adage that says, "Be careful what you ask for; you just might get it" is rather pertinent when wishing for something. My *Emotional Transformation: Learn to Speak the Language of Creation* CD teaches creating not out of the desire for a particular outcome but by using the emotion you would like to feel afterward.

Discernment Regarding Nonphysical Beings
Do *not* assume that simply because guidance is nonphysical that it is more evolved or knowledgeable than you are. In the nonphysical realms, as on earth, there are *all types* of energies and beings, some of which you would choose to hang out with and some you would steer a wide path around. Channeling is a vibration relationship, so be attentive to what kind of vibrational energy you are offering when you communicate in this way (and all the time!).

Choose to connect when you are feeling authentic and calm. When you are depressed, you attract energy that matches depression. Rely upon your intuition in all interactions. If it feels right, it probably is. Trust yourself. The vibrational law "like attracts like" can limit or assist you in reaching the levels you wish to access both in communication and in manifestation. If you aren't sure, practice discernment while remaining open to the guidance that your spirit guides so eagerly want to offer you.

Channeling Exercise
Review the "How to Channel" section on page 92, then get a pen and paper, and open yourself to receiving your guidance through writing what comes to mind after asking: Is there anything I need to know right now?"

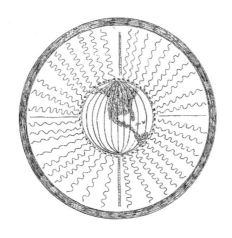

11. THE EARTH IN
CHRIST CONSCIOUSNESS

We are literally one with the earth. We live within her atmosphere, which is an integral part of the planet. When we breathe in, we breathe in Mother Earth; her substance has created every cell of our bodies. We simply borrow our bodies from her for our sojourn on earth.

Hope: How does a return to the earth coincide with Christ consciousness?

Jesus: As source energy incarnate, the earth is a sacred vessel of conscious expression of the One God. When an individual chooses the embodiment of the Christ consciousness on earth, he must find some expression for this as part of the earth system, part of the natural world. Saints and sages have always been closely connected with the earth, the animals, and plants. What a modern embodiment of the Christ consciousness will discover is that there is no separation between oneself and the earth. The earth, as part of the One, is oneself, and she comes a harmonious and cooperative substrate from which to create. So when one is attempting the impossible, which is

99

to define oneself as separate from the earth, he cuts himself off from his very source of life. This leads to disharmony and ultimately death.

The gift that the earth offers is as a teacher and fellow initiate—a teacher of perfect interrelationships and an initiate in the alignment with the Source that the earth demonstrates. There is nothing out of alignment with source energy on the earth that is natural (man-made things of the modern world are not included here). So, there *is* no separation; there can be no journey without the earth.

Our earth is home; we are connected deeply to her. Engaging in some way acknowledges her as our home and is what the Christ within calls for us to do.

A closer connection to the earth is perfect for cultivating our sense of unity with all things. Being in nature is healing. It calms our minds and resets us to the vibration our bodies were designed for. The artificial environments we live in increasingly separate us from the natural vibration of the earth. For example, electrical fields resulting from the fixtures separate us from the earth, as do appliances, computers, and wireless technologies, such as cordless house phones, cell phones, and wireless Internet connections. All of these may interfere with the communication of our cells, cell membrane function, and calcium metabolism. They also increase free radical production, creating cellular stress and premature aging and damaging our sense of well-being and health.[48] Now, too, the entire earth is covered with cell phones antennas. Add to that our perception that the earth is just "what we walk on" every day when we leave our homes rather than an integral part of our consciousness. These issues all combine to create a psychological, emotional, and energetic distance between the natural vibration of the living earth and us. The earth is alive and is affected by the toxicity that humanity creates on all levels.

---

48   Rees and Havas, *Public Health SOS: The Shadow Side of the Wireless Revolution*, 43.

I know from experience how much easier it is to see all as one and have a relationship with the natural world when walking through the woods as opposed to while riding the subway or spending time in the hubbub of the city. For me, it is a "level of stimulus" issue. When our five senses receive so much input, it can be hard to remain relaxed and internally quiet enough to hear inner guidance and the earth's whisperings in our lives.

In my book, *Where the Wisdom Lies: A Message from Nature's Small Creatures*, the small creatures of the earth speak about natural time versus artificial time. They say that our choice to follow our artificial clocks over Nature's natural time creates dissonance that is "causing the whole earth system to fall apart." Their point is that natural time and artificial time are irreconcilable rhythms and that our only choice to save the planet, life, and ourselves is to return to natural time. In Christ consciousness, we know the earth as ourselves and move within the natural vibration that she is, not foregoing the artificial clock time but encompassing the slower daily, monthly, and seasonal rhythms of nature into our lives. For example, the winter is a time for quiet regeneration and rest; spring brings renewal, energy, and growth; summer is for strengthening, practice, using energy wisely, gathering in groups, travel, and communication; and fall is the time for shedding what is unnecessary and gathering the harvest. Observing and living within these rhythms is one way to bring natural time into your life and cultivate your personal relationship with the earth.

Leonid Sharashkin, the English editor of the *Ringing Cedars* series, shares the roots of Russian words that link the journey of the spirit to the cycles of the seasons, to the care of the soil, and to the true role of humans as creators on earth.[49] According to Sharashkin, the Russian phrase for "kingdom of God" has origins that mean "family homestead inscribed in the natural cycle." *Chelove-vek*, Russian for "Man," means "eternal mind" or "wholeness." *Ra-Bota*, the word for "work," means "talking with the sun." *Lada*, the origin for "lady," means "goddess of universal love," and *Lud* means "manifestation

---

49   Sharashkin, *Ringing Cedars Workshop*.

of universal love." These words are a rich inspiration for a return to a spiritual connection with the earth.

No matter where you live, you can still consciously connect with the earth. Start by greeting her each morning as you leave your home, or love her as you step consciously upon her each day. Thank the earth before eating; gratitude prepares your body to receive the nutrients within the food. Sometimes I thank all the plants and animals that make up my meal before eating or I say: "Bless this food, the hands that prepared it, the farmers that raised it, the devas [nature spirits] that watched over it, and the earth that nurtured it, that it may bring perfect health to these vessels as we walk in the consciousness of the I AM, and may all who walk the earth be so blessed."

Relationship with the Earth
Our relationship with the earth is both *internal* and demonstrated by *how or where* we live. Ask yourself: *What is my relationship with the earth? What have I given the earth today? If I were the earth, what would I want from me?*

Spiritual Permaculture: An Idea for a New Way of Living
Jesus highlights how the earth is a teacher of perfect interrelationships. Permaculture is a design system that can be applied to gardens, farms, or communities; it uses natural ecosystems as a model to create beneficial relationships and to provide for human needs.[50] Permaculture systems are guardians of the earth. They are not just sustainable; they are regenerative. Their aim is to strengthen nature's systems.

Permaculture, also called forest gardening, works with nature; it doesn't resist it. For example, interplanting edible crops within existing landscapes minimizes maintenance and mimics natural ecosystems. Another Permaculture strategy is to create berms to slow the water's flow and passively direct it to fruiting trees. It uses strategies like multiple functions, where each part of the landscape serves more than one purpose, for example an herb, provides its

---

50 Whitefield, *How to Make a Forest Garden.*

leaves for cooking, a place for beneficial insects to live, and beauty in the garden. It uses redundancy, and problem solving in which the problem is viewed as the solution and the waste product of one system meets the needs of another part of the system. Permaculture is a local response to farming systems that have become monolithic, remote from consumers, and that rely on pesticides, chemical fertilizers, large machinery, and fossil fuels.

"Spiritual" or "sensitive Permaculture" takes Permaculture one step further and incorporates working with the spirit in all things.[51] This brings healing to the earth at an even deeper level because it adds spiritual healing to the physical healing in the earth's systems. The Findhorn Foundation in Scotland and the Perelandra Center for Nature Research in Virginia are two places that actively practice a conscious and interactive relationship with nature. When the plants, soil, microorganisms, and so on are treated as conscious forms, the interconnectedness of life and whole systems is strengthened, creating healing in the earth systems that have been damaged by Man's unconscious activities. Spiritual Permaculture is an example of bringing Christ consciousness literally "down to earth," as seeing all as one includes all life forms.

The Garden Elf

When I moved to the country, I wanted to create a vegetable garden and work with the energies of the land, so one day I leaned against a tree and opened myself to communicate, as it turned out, with the garden elves. The garden elves, in answer to my question of what their role is said, "We keep the balance of energies amid the many levels of life through harmonizing, redistributing, and controlling how it flows together." They said how grateful they were for the opportunity to work together: "You have no idea how wondrous and rare this is." I had a very long conversation with the garden elves that day. They said the first step in working together is to "agree that we wish to work with each other and lay down some guidelines so that we know what to expect of each other. Then we can set up our intentions for

---

51   Moore, *Sensitive Permaculture*.

the end result and allow the energies that are inherent in the intention (but latent) to do their work; we can assist them in birthing." They trained me in how to be in relationship with them, saying, "There is no work to be done without our consultation," and they asked that I greet them as I enter the garden. They explained, "There are many, many beings and levels of life, and it is appropriate to welcome and honor all life that seeks a comfortable place to create and be—much as you do. This sets a tone of congeniality, cooperation, and mutual respect that is critical to a venture such as this."

They said I needed to breathe more deeply and ground myself in the earth through my feet. They offered, "This is a basic guide for humans who need a gateway and a cleansing as they venture from the world indoors. You see, there is much disconnection from the earth inside; there is much shallow breathing. The great gift of human life is to bring together in one vessel (the human body) the physical and nonphysical; this you can do with grounding and breath."

They taught me how to create and suggested that rather than say to them (as I did), "I wish to create a fenced-in area for a new garden," instead I might consider "creating it in its physical, visual, emotional, and spiritual effect." To create in this way, means to see it in your mind's eye, feel the emotion it creates in you, and sense its spiritual energy. The elves pointed out that "the garden's species, structures, and such may be invited in through this envisioning; their energetic blueprint is created that way. You not only create all of these aspects of the garden in your mind's eye and your emotional body, but you also go beyond your own bodies to the place of all creation—a causal plane, where manifestation begins. You connect to this level energetically with pictures and feelings and spiritual centeredness."

I responded, "So, to create the garden, you want me to envision how I feel being in it, my joy in looking at it, the ease of maintaining and creating it, the abundant food of highest nutritional value that will come from it, and the fullness of my spirit in the process of its creation and in the resulting garden?"

"Yes!" they said. "Exactly!"

So I said, "I begin with gratitude for this land, all the life that exists here and makes it beautiful and whole. I am grateful for the creation of wholeness here that incorporates nature's whim and perfection, I add species and structures to enhance the whole, bringing greater diversity, color, abundance, and joyful expression. I see flowers, herbs, vegetables, trees, and bushes that are useful for human life, which feed not only the humans here but the land and its needs as well. I see a place where the land and the earth receive as much as they give. I see joy and ease expressed through the human and energetic co creators of this place. I feel deep satisfaction in knowing the interconnectedness of all life and in feeling like this co created garden is an expression of a new way of being on earth. I see people being attracted to this place to be healed, to learn these ways, and to share their gifts and creations. I see animals and new structures (barns perhaps). I see people and energies honoring and joyfully present."

They responded, "You are beginning now. *The process has begun.* The next step is feeding the creation with further energetic "juice" from all levels—emotionally, mentally, spiritually, and vitally: with physical energy."

I then asked them for their vision. They answered, "We see a land alive with all forms of life: insect, animal, bird, bee, plant, tree, bush, herb all of these myriad forms of life enlivening each other. We see the creation of this joyful abundant and boisterous overflowing of life that comes into creation with ease beyond all previous experience. (If it is otherwise, it is because you have created it thus.) We see a series of beds, raised if you wish, circular in pattern, that radiate outward and honor the four directions, the ancestors of the land, and all life. In honoring the life forms that lead up to the snail, the bee, the chicken, and the apple tree, by connecting to these ancestral foundations of life, we create a solid ground for new creation, design, and life. We see healing herbs in the center around a Genesa crystal (an energy generating form), signifying our joint intention of bringing healing to the center of all life. Then around the herbs, we see vegetables signifying the feeding of life, the full vibrant expression that is possible here in this Eden when land and sky are joined as one. Then beyond the circle, we see trees that bear fruit, rooted in the earth, stable and permanent, and bushes that have berries. They are symbols of the structure and stability that can come when life is whole and fed. They remind that a structure that supports and returns year after year is possible. Outside the fence will be fruits and berries planted solely for the wild creatures—the birds, deer, and rabbits—so that all life is fed and honored, not only man." I was bowled over by their description, and their structure was what I used to create the garden.

The garden elves assisted my intention for the garden to be realized while doing their very real work as part of nature's work force. In working with these energies of the land, we acknowledge that we are not the only species or consciousness that has an interest in the process or project. An amazing potential exists in this interface of human and nature consciousness. My challenge is in remembering to honor my agreements and to follow through at many levels, including practical, social, and energetic. Perhaps you can see how this relationship deepens and enriches the process of life and creation. This method of creation may be used for anything.

The following quote from the guides makes more sense in light of the garden elves explaining the depth of life that is part of nature's consciousness: "There once was a way of being on earth that honored this oneness, this knowing. The earth herself represented this union of all to the inhabitants here. The earth was the focus and the provider of all abundance (and still is), and she was honored in every moment, in every step, and in every action that the beings of that time took."

The Frontier of Earth Healing

Jesus healed people by seeing them as perfect. His highly coherent energy emanation (aligned in his body, mind, spirit, and divinity) overrode the less organized energy condition of the sick, and healing occurred. He didn't focus on their ailments—that would have only made the energy template for sickness stronger. He instead focused upon their innate perfection, creating—with their cooperation—the perfected human form that lay within their DNA.

This model for healing can be taken into the realm of earth healing as well. In the Gulf of Mexico and other places that have been polluted, the frontier for cleanup, in addition to the obvious physical cleanup, is energy and people themselves. When people gather, remotely or on-site, with aligned intentions and the understanding of the power they have simply as human beings to affect the world around them, anything is possible. If groups of people were focused on seeing the perfection innate within the natural world, they would reinforce this perfect template energetically and form the physical reflection of it. By seeing divine perfection within people, places, systems, and water bodies, humans have the capacity to heal. Imagine the result of many Christs working together in this way!

I remember that I can ask Jesus about his healings in the Bible, and he says,

> Yes, this is true. Furthermore, the healing occurred on the physical, emotional, and spiritual levels so that the entire being healed—not just the physical structure—for without healing the energetic template for the broken form (body), the body would revert to its former state. And what would be the point in that?

So, you see, the energetic creative component is the first and foremost tool for healing the body or the earth. I like your idea of gathering to heal the earth in this way, for it lays at your feet the very structure and substance of your species' survival. If the earth is honored and treated as the source of life and joy in great abundance, so much is possible for humans in the times ahead.

However, if she is ignored and devalued, there is little hope for humanity's future. So go forth with courage and claim the earth as your rightful and only home! Namaste. We are one.

Heaven on Earth

Stop here and imagine that your corner of the world is heaven on earth. Envision what is there physically; what does it look like? How does it feel? What is its spiritual effect? What might you do to create it? You set it in motion by, as the garden elves said, "feeding the creation with further energetic 'juice' from all levels—emotionally, mentally, spiritually, and vitally: with physical energy."

We have already begun to create heaven on earth!

12. THE CLEANUP DETAIL:
PHYSICAL, EMOTIONAL, MENTAL, SPIRITUAL

Well, we are almost at our destination in this guidebook. We have defined Christ consciousness, and we have learned that it is our human destiny. We've discovered that seeing all as one is really all we need to "do," and we've heard about the happiness and creativity it can bring. We have learned how to connect with our guidance and to the earth. But we haven't yet addressed the "unpacking list" mentioned in the preface: the unpacking list includes all parts of ourselves that are out of alignment with unity or Christ consciousness and that capture us in our human perspectives.

Congruence/Spiritual Integrity

> **Jesus**: Spiritual integrity is one's alignment with the spiritual values that one holds in life. The unity of all in spirit and the separation in form is misleading ... if the actions one takes are in alignment with the unity of all of life, one has spiritual integrity. In the spiritual world, there is no past, and no cleanup is required. At the human level, there is a past, and *if there are parts of your past that you are dragging along with you,*

go ahead and clean them up. Know that whatever actions you take in alignment with this intention to cleanup your past are multiplied a thousand times over. And that is all.

We operate from different "selves" in different areas of our lives. We are not all one self that is working toward one goal, and our many "I's," are at different levels of evolution and willingness. In order to bring myself into spiritual integrity, I need to have my "I's" aligned. This is challenging to say the least, because most of the I's are not particularly interested in the spiritual path, or spiritual integrity and don't wish to change. I have found that the "I" that I give voice to in any moment is the one that is strengthened. And so the spiritual path is one of not giving voice to the I's that would wish to be reactive, or selfish, or wounded by someone's actions, essentially overcoming, outwitting, and out waiting the many I's that keep me trapped and out of spiritual integrity. Finding and strengthening the voice of the self that is seeing all as one, is the best tool for this difficult task. This alignment is important because when parts of our lives are in conflict, it affects our energy levels and vibrational offerings.

Pilgrimage to Conyers

This reminds me of a time when I had just started on the spiritual path. I saw an article in the *New York Times* about Conyers, a small town outside of Atlanta, Georgia, where people saw an apparition of Mary, and pilgrims were gathering there. When I saw the article and photograph, I knew I had to go there. I didn't know why; I just knew I had to go. It was *way* outside of my comfort zone; my ego did *not* want anything to do with being a "pilgrim." But I bought a ticket to fly down to Atlanta in the morning and return in the evening. I rented a car and started driving east to Conyers. I didn't know exactly where in the town I was going, but since it was a small town, I had faith that I would be able to find it. Once in the town, I asked directions, of a man in a dry cleaning store, he didn't really know where it was, but he thought it was in "that" direction, pointing me down the main road. I drove and drove and didn't see anything. I was becoming worried, as there were fewer buildings, and I said out loud to my guide,

"Well, if you want me to get to this place, you have to help me find it!" At that point, I became aware of the car having turned onto a side road, and I was fifty yards down it by the time I realized what had just happened. The car had turned the corner and driven "itself"; it was as if I had disappeared for those moments.

A short ways down the road was a handwritten poster that said, "Pilgrim parking." This was it! I spent the day there, singing Spanish songs with the other pilgrims who were evidently devout Catholics. We gathered in front of a small house with a porch where the miracle was said to have occurred. Seeing me come and sit down on the grass among them, the other pilgrims gave me a sheet with the words they were singing and welcomed me in. There was a healing well that I gathered water from, following the steady stream of people walking there. I later returned home, empowered by having moved beyond my comfort zone in some mysterious and joyful way and by the miracle of the guides' intervention.

I share this story with you because I realized that my body, mind, and spirit could not remain in harmony if I didn't follow my spirit's command to make the trip. It was like there was no choice, and I was aware enough of wanting to be aligned that I was willing to do a very out-of-the-box thing to lift myself up to a standard that my spirit was calling me to. In some ways, it was like a graduation to another level or a test of sorts that I recognized as such and met with the egoic surrender that was required. I stepped forward to meet it. My body and mind fell (reluctantly!) in line with a demand from my spirit.

Who is My Master?
To be congruent in body, mind, and spirit, or to have spiritual integrity, we need to be able to answer the following questions: *Who is my master? Who or what am I in service to? What is my highest truth? Am I living that truth in all areas of my life? Are there parts of my life I need to bring into alignment with what I know to be true?* [52]

---

52   Hamilton, "The Evolutionary Life Transformation Program".

Physical

The following quote refers to the health laws of body, mind, and spirit: "When the pattern of thought is changed, the materialization of the pattern also changes. Obviously then, to produce a right result in matter, the pattern must be right. The bodies of some people never seem to change or show age. Why? Because they keep the pattern right by following the health laws of body, mind, and soul. Others change considerably because they disregard these laws; the pattern in the mind changes; or deteriorates, and the life force or power of God flowing through that pattern changes the body, or the materialization in matter."[53]

We create health for ourselves when we focus upon the perfection inherent within our bodies and support it with good food, exercise, clean water, fresh air, and all the other things that help us to be in vibrant health.

Jesus offers another ingredient for health.

> **Hope**: What supports Christ consciousness at the level of the physical body?

> **Jesus**: When one is in peak physical condition, one is in alignment with nature's dictates. Nature is a perfect example for the human in search of health and healing. Nature is never still, always in motion, and always adjusting to the seasons, the cycles, and the phases of the moon. There is never one day quite like the one before it or the one after it. This variability is nature's strength and her gift to the human on earth.

> When one truly knows and observes the land of her birth that she grows up on and lives on through her days, a relationship comes into being that is like friendship. She knows her trees like friends, and she knows where the different herbs grow, when the berries are in season to pick, and what animals will be where at any season and at any time of day. This intimacy with the earth brings true health and vitality to a human being.

---

53 Lewis, *"Can Thought Change Matter?"*, 55.

Peak conditioning is a bit daunting. Not since playing lacrosse in school have I been in peak condition! But remembering that Christ consciousness is already within me, I can work toward peak conditioning knowing that I can also call on the strength of the One as I need it. I have noticed when I do my morning exercises, the Five Tibetans (a series of exercises that have been called the fountain of youth, for their ability to energize the body). from within the perspective of seeing all as One, that the exercises become much easier because I become so much more, I become the whole room moving my body, instead of just my human form moving the body.

The Earth is Our Outer Body

Ask yourself, *Am I caring for my body well enough?*

In Christ consciousness, our definition of our body changes. The guides say "The earth is simply the outer body of you who live upon her. Treat her with love; allow her to feed you, clothe you, and to sustain your life. Honor her with your gratitude, your gift for her gifts."

Ask yourself, *Am I caring for the earth, my greater body, too?*

The Healing Bed

Jesus's statement that "intimacy with the earth brings true health and vitality" is something I discovered firsthand. I had just returned from a transformative two weeks in Hawaii with Kahu Abraham Kawai'i. I was in a pretty high-energy state. I lay down on the lawn to look at the stars, and after awhile I got a "download." My awareness instantly accessed a complete package of information. The downloaded information was for "the healing bed," a bed dug eighteen inches into the earth that I was to lie in for three hours a day. I rushed inside and wrote it all down. Several days later, I carefully selected a location, built a wood frame to make the sides stable, and dug a hole that deep to lie in. Yes, it *did* look very much like a grave, and thankfully, the neighbors couldn't see the spot I chose! I really did lie in it for three hours each day for several days that first week and then, though not usually for three hours at a time, I consistently lay in it each day for several months after that. I found that I felt really safe and that I could relax at a whole new level. The healing bed gave me a totally different feeling from lying on top of the ground. As I used it over time, I developed cellular awareness, I could feel each cell in my body. I was calmer and more in tune with what my body needed in the way of food and movement. I had to figure out a new way of eating because I craved fresh live foods and couldn't tolerate eating my usual diet.

Emotional

Hope: What supports Christ consciousness on the emotional level?

Jesus: Emotions are the flag that blows in the wind of our centeredness. When we are calm, centered, and connected, our flag and its movement are within our control. Our emotions are authentic responses to actual conditions. They healthily release energy, make connections, and heal through radiant, unconditional love. The converse—emotions that come from a stressful, reactive, or preprogrammed state—are quite different in their effect. Not only do they harm, interfere, and disconnect, but also they are unhealthy for the organism and the earth.

Now, how is one to find the harmony and balance to support healthy emotions?

Begin with now. Are you breathing? How does your body feel right now?

When we get caught up in external happenings and stimuli, we get tense and lose our connection with the core of our beings. The practice of a spiritual path is simply this:

becoming simultaneously aware of our inner and outer states as we interact.

It's kind of interesting that to control our emotional states, we look at our bodies.

Tension in the body comes when the outer world sucks us into exclusive focus on it at the expense of the inner world. The spiritual path is to be aware of both. We cannot be present for our Christ selves when we are reactive, angry, over stimulated, or emotionally drained. Simply returning to your breath throughout the day can help you find peace and stillness, even if the world around you is in turmoil.

You may have noticed that emotional reactivity is not the easiest thing to clean up! Give yourself some margin for setbacks here. I have had some really strong backlash from my ego. I have felt like the monster from the black lagoon has attached itself to my chest and covered me with gray slime. However, the amazing thing that I am realizing is that I can still choose to act from the vision of oneness *even if I feel the ego's attachment to me.* It's not easy (and I can't yet to do it every time), but I am not held hostage in the same way I used to be.

There is a place for all emotions in our world, and we needn't judge ourselves for having them. In fact, accepting that we do have them makes it easier to see all as one, a task that is difficult when we just want to include the "good" parts of ourselves and leave all other parts out. When we realize the emotions we feel are part of the human condition, they can become less personal. You needn't judge yourself or draw conclusions by their presence in your life. They come and they go, and you can say with a yawn, "Ho, hum, there you are again!" As we remain centered and watch our breath, it gets easier to observe emotions from the impersonal perspective of unity consciousness, which can transform them. It's like their volume is turned down, loosening their grip on our lives.

I remember reading the definition of a spiritual master somewhere: a master is one who leaves no word unsaid, and no misunderstanding to dangle until next time. Make a practice of leaving a clean emotional trail as you move through your days, and the rest will take care of itself. One way to check your trail is to ask yourself, *If I die now, am I at peace in all my relationships?*

Love's Many Faces

It doesn't seem right to move on from this section on emotions without touching on love, the most powerful of all human emotions and the reflection of divine love.

> **Hope**: Jesus, please help me to understand the emotion of love in our world. Can you speak about love and its many faces?

> **Jesus**: Yes, dear one. It is with grace and joy that this question alights in my today, for there is much misunderstanding about love and its role and ruses. For example, the way to love is a many fingered path, for there are ways to embrace love that are far from what we would think looks like love.

> There are loves that have an almost masochistic flavor, for they hold an individual to a deep internal path of self-revelation and inquiry.

> What love's grace offers most is light, joy, and understanding— that quickening of the heart; that ease in the being. Love dwells in this face most divinely.

> One can know love by the outcome of its action. For example: when love is hard and demanding, yet the outcome is greater order, alignment, and the ability to stand in truth, then this is love.

> When love looks like it doesn't care and is aloof, this too can manifest eagerness and willingness that all the standing and whipping in the world couldn't elicit.

> When love is understanding and kind, the other being is opened and vulnerable and feels like he can go on, do more, and be more just through its kind touch.

The faces of love are limitless, and in the embodiment of the Christ consciousness, this is an excellent query, for the limitation of love is the limiting of life, as well.

If your only response is of kindness and caring, then you limit and see only a fraction of love's possibility. In the old days, the demand to defend yourself, your town, or your country was an act of love, as well, for saving and protecting life and life forms could not have happened otherwise. The other life forms that would take over your land and your ways of living would cut short your chance to love![54]

So this isn't an invitation to do what you please and call it love. It is an invitation to see through the action you take to its reception in the world, in the other. See what it creates in its immediacy and down the road, and then you can decide if it is true love. Only then can you be sure of your gift or your curse to another. So the thinking through of love's action to its landing in the heart, mind, and soul of another is an important way to determine its efficacy and thus its worthiness for someone manifesting Christ consciousness.

As God speaks and acts and loves through you, only surety and confidence come. As you love in the way of discipline and hardness, you will feel confident, for you will hold the soft edge to that discipline that lets through the love that is fragile and kind into the other's heart. The one you love will sense your caring, your concern, and your wish for the highest outcome in her life.

This, too, is possible in your relations with yourself. When you love yourself through applying discipline to your actions, you create great possibilities in your life. Think of those things that you know are good for you but that you find hard

---

54　What Jesus means here is that: The other people that would take over your land and kill you would cut short your chance to love, and thus it is within the bounds of "loving" to protect that right to love by defending your land and life.

to do and continue day after day—those are love in action. These are God's loving presence in your life, your initiation to love through the one and only being that all are. Your willingness and awareness that this thing that has been hard is in truth love can change *everything* about it. So this has answered your question, we[55] trust?

Hope: Yes, thank you. That was eloquent!

This is a useful guide as a parent. It is reassuring to know that love can be so many things, and still be love: graceful, hard, demanding, aloof, understanding or kind. The bottom line is *the outcome of love's action*: ease, order, ability to stand in truth, alignment, eagerness, willingness, opening, vulnerability, ability to keep going, or do more and be more.

Mental

Hope: What supports Christ consciousness mentally?

Jesus: The mind is a great resource, for without it, there is no possibility for creation. The mind, however, is man's deepest fault, as well, for it is untrained and difficult to direct at will. So the trick is to watch the mind, to watch the actions that the mind chooses, and get cleverer than it is. Find its niches of exposure, where it is vulnerable to direction, and take advantage in those places. For example, when a person is ill at ease and observes the mind and its dance of reasons (for being ill at ease), there is an opening. When a person sees the mind in a new state, she has an opening. These openings are critical to the observer and must be utilized repeatedly and consistently to untangle the fiendish mind's workings. Your mind would have you at its beck and call, but the path homeward is that you are the master and not the servant of your mind.

---

55   Jesus sometimes uses "we", in our communications. In the consciousness of the One, "we" is as natural an expression as "I".

Patterns of thought are what you must observe. Now, once these patterns have been seen in the light of day and you have found ways to catch them at their source, then the real opportunity exists to forge new pathways in the brain to higher ways of being on the earth. By "higher," we mean states in which there are more possibilities, more choices for your actions. So once you see all the choices possible, you have attained mastery. Ask yourself, *Could I love right now? Am I present right now? Could I offer myself right now?* If you ever answer "no" to any of these questions, you must examine your placement in the continuum of All That Is and see that there is more work to be done. In all situations, all choices must be at your disposal.

What this means, as well, is that your body is not determining or limiting either your choices or your emotions, for that matter. They must all be within your control and direction. Full mastery of the self is required for the full embodiment of the Christ consciousness. "Full mastery" sounds quite daunting, quite difficult, but in truth, what this involves is not a discipline in the traditional sense, but a discipline in reverse of sorts: a discipline that does not create a rigid line of movement or focus and that does not demand a certain way or outcome. The new discipline is holding at bay the patterns of behavior that demand a certain way of being to affect an end.

For example, you enter a room filled with new people. Your old way of discipline is to do as you have been taught, to do what is socially appropriate in greeting and touching people as you feel it is right. In the new way, you might arrive in a room and allow your actions to be completely different every time you do so. Predictability is the hallmark of a being captured by convention and old thought patterns. Unconventionality and spontaneous action that is new and appropriate in its spontaneous assessment of the situation calls forth from you and all of those around you a new offering of how to be in a room together.

This means that not only are the old rules, ways, and authority figures unnecessary, but that when you do these actions by rote and not by paying attention to the moment's truth, you feel a loss of energy. When this occurs, you will know you have made progress on the road to mastering a new way of being.

Your mind's journey is the most challenging for some. The truth of it is that there is no one way, no right way. However, knowing the end goal *of all choices in every moment* will guide you in the way that is best suited to your journey. Not only will you find your way there [to the mastery of your mind] but also you will find others who will journey there with you if you are clear in your intention and in offering your permission to your guidance system to assist you to this goal. Namaste. We are one.

So what Jesus is saying is that our minds are our most important tools, and they must be retrained. We must observe them to find the moments when our thoughts are changing. In these moments, we see our minds' habitual *actions*. Once we have discovered our habitual thoughts and do not automatically cede to them, we are then able to be authentic in every new moment. This gives us more choices.

Meditation is a process that assists us in seeing our minds in action. Most of us don't realize the extent to which our minds whip us around through life. My mind is like an overactive monkey—at times, it is here, there, back and forth; it does not stay with anything very long. This becomes obvious when sitting in meditation. Meditation has been a huge help to see this "critter" in action and realize how much wasted energy results from my overactive mind's condition.

Meditation Exercise

In meditation I sit, and my mind rushes off with me. I am lost in thought until I realize it—"Oh"—and come back to meditating. I sit in stillness for a nanosecond or two, sinking into a place of non-thought until my mind whips me off onto another tangent without my noticing it. I am lost in different thoughts until I notice and return again to meditating. This goes on and on, over and over. The only thing that determines its effectiveness is how often I am able to catch myself and return to meditation, and my *willingness* to do it (it takes some effort to pull myself away from my mind's thoughts). When I eventually see the patterns of thought that my mind enjoys, they lose their power over me. When we stop believing our own thoughts, there is space in our minds for stillness. Meditating with a group can be a very powerful assistance because the coherent field of energy that the group creates as it sits with a shared intention and focus helps quiet the mind and create a greater ability to remain still.

If you have tried meditation and found it tedious, you are right! You might try it again with the realization that once you get over the resistance to sitting, meditation ends up feeling like food for the spirit and you will wonder how you managed without it for so long.

Stop here for a moment and meditate for five minutes. Sit on the floor on a cushion or on the front edge of a firm chair. Put your hands comfortably on your knees or thighs. Keeping your spine straight allows the energy to move freely up and down your spine. Gently close your eyes almost all the way. Breathe, and observe your breath.

Did you experience difficulty in sitting? It may take more than five minutes to move beyond the resistance we have to being still. Sometimes it takes me twenty minutes to finally surrender to sitting and being, and sometimes I can't seem to surrender at all.

Spiritual

Hope: What supports Christ consciousness spiritually?

Jesus: When one intends Christ consciousness, there is no way not to ultimately achieve it. The intention demonstrates a clear knowledge that this intention is the choice of the One in question. When individuals choose this goal as the overriding vision for life on the level of the spirit's journey, they give themselves (in the greater sense) the permission to be led there. This is the singular most effective step toward the embodiment of this consciousness that there is. Nothing in the way of trying this or that will offer what this intention will in the way of movement toward this goal.

When the child of God says, "I wish to embody the God force on earth that I may fully express the joyful ways of life here on this planet," there is rejoicing in the heavens, for there is much that the heavens receive from this child of God's intention on earth. The life force that makes you live is one that not only pours forth from our level to you, but it also returns to us out of an expansion of your thoughts, words, and deeds. Levels of energy not before manifested on earth create a great cycle of movement and creative force. Yes, force, the life force …

When individual souls come into human bodies, they do so in order to make manifest the Divinity on earth. A being who knows this consciously, moves in this direction, and actually offers himself as a conduit for this level of light is fulfilling his intention of earthly embodiment.

So when one says to oneself in a moment of quiet and focus, "My goal is to embody the Christ consciousness on earth," the heavens open and offer all the materials to assist this to happen in one's life.

Can you picture a streambed clogged with debris, old sticks, dead leaves, and such? When one offers oneself to the goal of Christ consciousness, there is an increase in the energy flow ... the water gets faster and stronger, and much of the debris may be washed away. One in the Christ consciousness must offer a clear streambed, uncluttered with old, useless thoughts, patterns, ideas, or ways of being in the body. The increase in energy has a cleaning out effect in one's life. Be sure that what is cleaned out was meant to go and that what remains is more open, clear, and able to hold more water (i.e. Christ light).

So there it is, the one step that is required to set in motion the goal of Christ consciousness. Have faith in your guidance team. They know what needs to go if you don't. They will find ways to access and remove it, and you will thank them later.

All beings on earth will ultimately offer this as their goal; those of you who offer now are in the first wave of people moving in this direction. You pave the way and have much support from the unseen levels. Know this and be strong in your commitment to move forward as you are guided to. As you instincts lead you, go. Namaste. We are one.

Jesus refreshingly states that in setting our intention to embody our Christ selves, we cannot fail! In honestly choosing this as the vision for our lives, we give our guidance permission to lead us to people, places, situations, and practices that will make it happen.

I had not realized that we bring joy to the nonphysical world, which also benefits from our path to Christ consciousness. But we *are* a mechanism for growth, creativity, and expansion, and what we create naturally feeds the spiritual levels! This highlights for me the grand view of the One's great organism and its joyful movement to discovery and expansion. The life energy that pours from the Divinity to the earth returns to the Divinity as the engine of expansion, creating a great cycle of energy and creative life force. Through co-creation, more energy becomes available to us.

So, if this sounds like a choice you are ready to make, then at a time when you are centered and internally still, light a candle or create a small ceremony to say to your greater self, "My goal is to embody the Christ consciousness." When you do this, the heavens will shift into action, and you will be assisted in situations that help you to clear up things in your life that don't support your goal. More energy will move through you and into your life. Thought patterns, old stories, ideas. and habits will be made visible for you to examine and release. This requires willingness on your part; it doesn't "get done" *for* you! Your spirit's evolution is intimately tied to your ability to stick to your intended path. Stick to your commitment to free yourself! Release your old ways to make room for the new! Jesus assures that whatever gets thrown out needs to go, so don't look back or second-guess!

In summary, the unpacking list and the cleanup detail include the parts of your past you are dragging along with you. As you release the old voices—the "I's" that only know separation, limitation, and the story of the "little me" —you make room for your Christ self. You become spiritually integrated when you are aligned with the spirit at all levels of your life's expression.

Physically, we strive for "peak" condition, which is the result of following the health laws of body, mind, and soul and keeping our patterns of thought clean. When we add intimacy with the earth to this, we have true health, vitality, and life!

Emotionally, being aware of our breathing and bodies helps us remain calm, centered, and connected. This state is the perfect haven for the Christ self to shine forth.

Mentally, we must see the mind's patterns to extricate ourselves from its "fiendish" hold upon our lives. We have openings to do this when we observe the places where our minds change direction; at these moments, we have the opportunity to see what triggers our habitual thought patterns. When we no longer rigidly believe what we think, our minds become our servants instead of our masters. This then brings us the opportunity to have "all choices in all situations."

Spiritually, we simply need to state our intention to embody Christ consciousness and surrender to the process of transformation that follows. There are some difficult things to let go of as we unpack, but the things we leave behind become much less interesting when we see the unified world in front of us!

13. TRANSFORMATION TO CHRIST CONSCIOUSNESS

Recently, I had another session with Mary, my friend and spiritual healer. It seemed fitting to visit her as I was concluding the book, since a visit to her was my impetus for writing it. Seeing her was like getting an infusion of the Christ light.

The guidance, through Mary, reminded me that everything in my life has come through my consciousness: everything is a result of thoughts I have had. My thoughts broadcast out of me, collect like energy, and reflect back into my life. So I must *own* everything I have created and realize there is no appearance I cannot change!

I was encouraged to observe my mind in action, to allow no thought to come unsolicited, and to not engage with thoughts that are not of divine investment. It was suggested I say, "Peace, be still, and know that I am God" and that throughout the day I should remind myself of the truth of what is real, saying, "I am divinely creative consciousness."

Divinely Creative Consciousness
Try this for yourself and see what happens

The separation from my son and now former husband that I described in the beginning of the book has eased greatly, in many ways it feels unified and healed. We have been able to keep many of the good parts of what we had as a family, and evolve the rest…a wholeness has returned which feels right. We spend some weekdays together and many vacations. My son is with me on the weekends which gives my former husband time alone too. The emotional patterns that kept me in a jail of my own making, have been broken apart and our time together is much more harmonious. In seeing all as one, and by aligning (and realigning) with my spirit's purpose (not my ego's) a miracle is occurring in my life, and I am deeply grateful. New levels of seeing the perfection in the process of life grace my days.

The transformation to Christ consciousness is a *process* during which I am either in Christ's consciousness or human consciousness. One or the other—straddling doesn't work. Embodying the Christ is a choice I need to remake in every moment. Certain ongoing practices help me to be conscious enough to move in that direction: being in the present moment, daily meditation, doing the seeing all as one exercise, checking in with my guidance regularly and having a group of like-minded people to share the path with. There are days where everything flows beautifully, and there are days where I wish the job of moving beyond the ego's patterns was easier. Many times I have pleaded, "Just take me now; I can't stand myself anymore!" As of yet, no chariots have swung down out of the sky to carry me "home." I now realize that the pleading can only come from the separate self. But I still wonder, can I be the Second Coming "myself," or must transformation to Christ consciousness come in God's timing and not by my will?

Hope: Jesus, is transformation within our power, or must it come from an external stimulus?

Jesus: Transformation is when the delineation between oneself and the world shatters. This means that the definition of "who one is" completely changes. The "transformation" that is the difference between knowing the self as the isolated individual and knowing the self as the energy of All That Is incarnate.

The challenge is to translate that knowing, that transformed self, into its fullest expression—translating, if you will, the unification of All That Is as the One into the life of the individual. This is the challenge and the joy of life.

So life's joy is figuring out what translating Christ into my life means and then taking action to give it its fullest expression, which may put me outside my comfort zone![56]

Change versus Transformation

It is worth looking at the difference between change and transformation. Think of a napkin and all the ways you can fold it. That's change. Light it on fire. That's transformation! "Change" is self-improvement. It is easy to initiate and sometimes hard to maintain, as any dieter will attest. Being good at change helps you to sit loosely in the saddle of life—a good skill in preparing for transformation.

"Transformation" is when nothing of the old remains—we are not who we were before. Opening to Christ consciousness transforms us to being so much more! On the road to transformation, we can state our intention, set our compass, practice seeing and loving all as one from the perspective of our highest selves, and surrender to what is.

In transcribing the channel, I realized that Jesus didn't really answer the question, "Is transformation within our power?" So, I asked for clarification on how transformation occurs and the role of divine grace. (When Jesus mentions a "life stream" he means a human life.)

Jesus: Dear one, we are grateful for your inquiry: is it possible to enact this sometimes-chaotic reorganization of a life stream for oneself? There is never one way to do things on this earth; the beauty of this work of human life is its variety and the fact that no two people think or enact the process of life in

---

56 Hamilton, "The Evolutionary Life Transformation Program".

129

the same way. So the answer is really yes and no. Depends. Does that help?

Hope: Yes and no! So the action of grace is sometimes the impetus and sometimes not?

Jesus: Yes, you could say that. For how would you define grace? Couldn't an event of great difficulty, such as the burning down of one's home, be termed "grace"? The resulting outpouring of love and generosity from a community might precipitate transformation in a being, so the community could see the unified response of a single organism in action and thus be transformed itself.

Or would you limit grace to divine acts of mystery? Would you limit grace to when an individual finds a peeling back of her perception to include only the true essence of who she really is, and this exposure of truth comes from an inner willingness that no real event in life made occur? What if a life stream's vision of a new world precipitated a shedding of the old ways that she had clung to and a full embracing of the possibility of living in a completely different outer world? Couldn't this too be termed transformation?

So, in truth, there is only one—got you here! And there is no outer that transforms the inner or vice versa.
Hope: You are making me smile with that one. I had fallen for my own argument; my vision had dropped into the separated version of me. Thank you!

So, really you could say that transformation is occurring all around us all the time, that what nature is doing at the end of the growing season, withdrawing life energy into the bulbs in the ground and the green tops dying back, is transformation, a regular rhythm of the earth. The growth of children, too, could be one transformation after the next—the letting go of one stage and allowing something else … I am getting excited about this one! If we would let the true miracle that life is move through us without fear or clinging, we would be transforming all the time! Is that right?

Jesus: Yes, you could say that. Transformation is an organic process in your world. The true vision for transformation to Christ consciousness, the dynamite explosion that catapults one to see through the eyes of unity consciousness, is never limited by anything that is not of the human being's making. Transformation is. Period. It is waiting outside your door, wanting to sweep you up and carry you into a life that is so much more! It is only those human attributes I mentioned that limit its expression in your life.

Hope: Thank you; that makes it quite clear. I see a gorilla sitting outside the door ready to come in ...

Jesus laughs, and then he continues.

Jesus: Oh, I like that picture! But it is not a gorilla to fear; it is a gorilla to play with—but at the gorilla's level of play, with strength and extreme unlimited potential. Do you see the distinction?

Hope: Yes, I think so. A powerful force would sweep us into action and ways of being that have great power within them, but only if we only allow the force in.

Jesus: Yes. Namaste. We are one.

The Gorilla of Transformation

So, I sit here and sip my tea. It's 5:30 a.m., the wind is howling outside, and I wonder, *What would I have to let go of to let the gorilla into my life to play?*

Perhaps you might like to make a cup of tea for yourself and ponder this question, too!

The Path Is Changing

The beauty of the times we are now in is that *so many* of us are undergoing transformation (by fire: divorce, financial ruin, job loss, sickness, environmental catastrophe, etc.). Life's difficulties are our spirits' opportunities, because they initiate a process that forces us to look beyond the physical world alone. We begin seeking greater meaning and spiritual connection in our lives. We are *all* being called to the path of transformation. Admittedly, some are being called to the path louder than others, but the beauty of this mass impulse is that the path is now a road—maybe even a highway—with monasteries, vegan restaurants, yoga studios, retreat centers, meditation groups, Internet classes, ashrams, gurus, teachers, and guidebooks along the way! No longer must we surrender everything to answer this call to the One. We may now embrace our spiritual selves and weave their depth into the fabric of our everyday lives.

The traditional path of spiritual attainment through ascetic or monastic life in remote locations is no longer necessary. We are being asked to be in the world and to bring what was available in the monastery or the cave into our existing lives. We carry the quiet connection within us as we actively engage in life.

The Earth Is Changing

The earth herself, our outer body, is also going through transformation now. Whether or not we are the cause of it, we face greater variability and extremes in weather, thinning of the ozone layer, global warming, earthquakes, tsunamis, solar flares, and other monumental disturbances of nature. Add to that social unrest and instability in governments, financial institutions, monetary systems, transportation networks, food production, and energy and water supplies, and we see a very insecure future. The interconnectedness of the earth's natural systems and systems that support human populations renders our position vulnerable at this time. We are all one, and the world, as portrayed on the front page of the newspaper, sometimes looks like it's a house of cards propped up with bamboo poles, and a stiff wind is on the way.

Chaos can be a necessary state between levels of organization. As chaos envelops our world, a tremendous opportunity awaits our every choice. Our choices will determine whether the earth moves toward greater unity or falls apart. The world is calling for our loving engagement and beckoning us to make our choices based on knowing we are all one.

> **Jesus**: A higher possibility is held out for us now. We have the vision beneath us of a world transformed, a world in unity, love, and alignment with divine law and natural law. There is no holding Man back from a rebirth of magnificent proportions. Not only is this what is needed for our blessed earth to recover her own health, but also the human species, back from the precipice of annihilation by our own hand, may too find rebirth and a hopeful future. Not knowing what might come next in the world outside of ourselves, our only choice is to look within to find a star by which to guide our ship. The transformation of the earth will come one being at a time, and you, dear reader, are being asked to step forward to make this happen. May your way be clear, your resolve strong, and your strength paramount as the journey unfolds. Namaste. We are one.

Journey's End

Well, I had hoped that by the time we arrived at the end of this guidebook together, I would be able to walk on water and practice bilocation! But not yet! I do have moments of seeing all as one, when the energy of the Christ self shines into my doing and being. The creative, expansive, unlimited, and unfettered self gets to come out and play a bit more. I am seeing how I can choose to look through Christ eyes, and what I have discovered is that it leaves the perspective of the "little me" in the dust. It is like inhabiting a brand new world; what I see is the same, but the meaning I make from it is different in the most profound way: I am surrounded by consciousness in its many expressions and forms, and we all meet as equals on this stage of earth.

The moments I embody the Christ within are those moments when I am surrendered, present, and humble enough to be available to something greater than myself. And it really boils down to my choosing what I will focus on in this moment: separation or unity? As the moments that are "mine" to choose increase, very slowly a Christ is freed! As more of us find our way to the Christ within, the world around us will have to change to reflect the higher order of unity consciousness. Imagine what kind of a world we will create from this place!

The Dragons of Separation

A future storybook will begin ...The world in crisis was created from a human population that was blind to the divine light present within them. As humans awakened to the Divinity within themselves, their inner human landscapes were revealed, with their very real maze of tunnels filled with memories, ideas, dreams, and misunderstandings about the world. The tunnels were guarded by the dragons of the illusion of separation. By courageously exploring their our own inner landscapes and one by one taming the dragons, they discovered hidden within themselves their own divine nature, trapped and waiting to be set free! Joining forces with their powerful and newly freed divine nature, they looked outward to the earth, knowing that they *were* all that they saw, and *that* changed everything.

As we arrive at the guidebook's destination, I ask Jesus if he would to paint a picture of this new world for us.

> **Jesus**: Yes, of course, my dear. The world that you can imagine is a bold and bright place of extreme joy and understanding or extreme opportunity and delight. When the Christ is present in the eyes, ears, hands, and feet of those lucky humans who walk the earth, the world becomes a benevolent place, a place of joyful interacting, clarity, and exuberant creative energy. When this occurs, life will be changed, for all life on earth and the earth herself will heal, and ... the land will be reborn anew.

My hope is that a conglomeration of those people willing to embody this level of the Divinity within will gather and create what might not have been even thought of before. In this vein, anything is possible, and all paths are of the Christ.

Go in peace, for only the land will hold you in her beautiful stillness that will bring you to new possibilities of an earth reborn and brand new. Namaste. We are one.

Here we have reached the guidebook's destination. Now is your opportunity to explore the landscape that lies within you and before you. With the Christ present in your "eyes, ears, hands, and feet" "life will be changed, for all life on earth and the earth herself will heal."

Thank You

Jesus: Thank you for your presence here with me until now. It has been a journey into the mind of a Christ. Perhaps you may see yourself in this role; perhaps it is not yet for you. Either way is fine. What is most important and what you will find is a sense of empowerment in the journey of your life: seeing how you can direct your journey and make it more of what you had in mind when you came. Perhaps this sense of creative energy will hold you up through difficult times when you remember, "Oh, yes! I can make a difference here for myself simply by focusing on what I *do* want." This will be enough for most as they walk though the pages of time. This is a fine and precious gift.

For those who would wish for more, there is treasure here beyond imagining—not to be cast aside but to be read and reread, for there are levels of understanding that can be gleaned upon a second and third reading of this work. Try not to be discouraged as the life patterns creep in and still exist over and over; simply hold yourself as the Christ that you are when you remember to, and your way will be empowered, the light of God will shine down upon the path you tread, and your way will be clear. Namaste. We are one.

Appendix A

Exercises to Loosen the Egoic Perspective and Expand the Realization That the Christ is within "You"
It can be difficult to jump from the view of the world that shows us amid separate things to embracing that entire world as ourselves. Practicing these exercises may help you to realize an expanded definition of who you are.

There is no one way to approach this topic; what is helpful, however, is the willingness to change and the understanding that you are much more than you ever realized or thought possible—not in an egoic sense but in a true reality sense of where your body ends and the world begins. Try to attend to these exercises once a day, and you will find great benefit and fun in them, too!

Exercise 1: Becoming One with Yourself
Stand in front of a large mirror. Look at yourself as though you were looking at someone else; with fresh eyes, see yourself. Say to your reflection, "I love you." Say this repeatedly, with meaning, until you can truly mean it, until you can truly feel it. If this isn't easy, do it each day until you are consistently successful. Claiming yourself as one worthy of being loved allows you to love others. (This exercise has been adapted from one practiced at a workshop with Kahuna Harry Uhane Jim.)

Exercise 2: Becoming One with Your Ancestors
Let's look at our ancestors for a moment. It is upon their efforts that our lives stand. They have toiled for our benefit and for the opportunities that we are now blessed with. Regardless of whether you even know (or like) any of them, they are still your ancestors, and

in some mysterious way, you must accept them in order to claim your full self here on earth. When you become one with your ancestors, you are then able to become one with yourself and your own children. From personal healing comes healing for our society and the earth.

The Exercise
In a quiet place where you will be undisturbed, picture yourself in a mirror. Then imagine your mother behind your left shoulder with her hand on your shoulder and your father behind you on the right with his hand on your right shoulder. Feel them. Then picture your parents behind you with their mothers and fathers behind them in the same way. Now you have six people standing behind you. Feel them. And then add their parents behind them ... expand from you to your parents to four grandparents, eight great grandparents, etc.. Feel them. Then visualize all your ancestors before them, creating a huge body of people standing behind you, supporting you, upon whose efforts and lives you stand. Regardless of your perceived difficulties with your parents, envisioning this connects you with the energy and power of their lives. Claim yourself as one of a part of the many. Thank them and ask for their support in all that you do. (Adapted from Bert Hellinger's family constellation work.)

Exercise 3: Wide-Angle Vision
Work each day toward seeing with your whole eye, widen or expand your focus to include everything you see. Don't focus on anything, while seeing everything in front of you. Seeing with the whole eye gives you a multitiered awareness of not only what is out there but also your body's position and your connection to the earth simultaneously. I learned this while attending a camp run by the Children of the Earth Foundation (CotEF).

Exercises 4–10 were given to me in the woods. (A story for another day!)

Exercise 4: Breathing Exercise
Breathe with whatever is around you (the chair, car, ground, etc.), in and out, and have it become a part of you. When you participate in

the web of existence, you change what is and connect with a greater whole. I find that when I do this, I begin to love that thing that I breathe with, and my heart expands in gratitude.

Exercise 5: Relax Like a Log
Lie down on a flat or inclined rock, the floor, the bed, or the couch. Starting from the head, move progressively down the body until you are completely relaxed, let go completely. This creates a complete internal release, freeing blockages that hold excess fluids, tension, and harmful thoughts.

Exercise 6: Spine Rolling
Align yourself with a wall, rounded upright pole, or smooth tree trunk, and then roll side to side against it, massaging and stimulating your back and spinal column. This helps the nerves, bones, and body to be healthy, creates flexibility, and connects you to the tree and All That Is. Do two to three times daily.

Exercise 7: Sensing into the Earth
Lie down on the ground and sense into the earth. What is beneath your sight? Is it rock, soil, water, floor? What is there? Relax, yet be open and aware. Using your extra sensory awareness search around a bit. Work toward openness to receive and to sense outward, actively projecting your awareness to a larger area around you. This is therapeutic and hones your ability to find lost things.

Exercise 8: Ashes to Ashes
Lie down on the ground and untie all tight clothing. Loosen your belt and shoes. Be still, completely still, so that your breath hardly moves. Imagine the leaves falling over you, the moss growing up around you, and the squirrels skittering over you, unnoticed. Do this as long as you can (on a blanket maybe). This relaxes you, renews your energy, and puts life in perspective.

Exercise 9. New Eyes Exercise
First go to a new place. Walk around while observing how you look at things, how you sense with your nose, eyes, skin, feet, and hands.

Then go to a familiar place and do the same thing. What difference do you notice when you see, feel, taste, and hear a familiar place through new perspective? You can pass time in this way if you are in a place where you are stuck (like a sickbed). You can transform routine places, relationships, and jobs in this way. Your life can be transformed when you see with new eyes.

10: The Invisible Exercise

Melt into the white space between the words on a page or the space between objects in a room. Simply open your cells to the outer substance, so that you are transmuted and transformed by resonance into that alternate substance. By your focus upon the space, you energetically align with it, and your cells resonate with the space that you are focused upon. Thus opening your outer skin cells and then each of the body's cells to become what is outside of you—(according to the source of the exercise not my first hand experience) this will shift you into the formless space if you are able to feed the cells with your focus and concentration long enough to create the new form for your body and hold it. Try this at a party or in a group, and see if anyone bumps into you to confirm your success!

11: Energy Balancing Exercise

Imagine yourself up above your house or apartment; look down upon it and relax your eyes, mind, and body. Scan your living areas with the intention of seeing them energetically. Notice areas of clear energy and areas of congested energy. I went up above the roof and looked down. You can do it floor by floor or the whole thing at once. Any area that comes to your attention, you can go in more closely to look at and find out why. When I did this, I noticed two areas of concern: both were where things were cluttered and disorganized. This is an excellent way to confirm the accuracy of your sight, afterwards you can confirm your finding in your own home, and remedy the situation.

About the Author

Hope Ives Mauran is a translator of wisdom from other dimensions. She has written *Where the Wisdom Lies: A Message from Nature's Small Creatures* and an audio CD, *Emotional Transformation: Learn to Speak the Language of Creation.* She is an artist of eco-spiritual modified landscapes, a teacher of Practical Pendulum 101 and a co-teacher with Martha Hamilton Snyder of intuition, guidance and messages from within.

Photo by Maggie Heinzel-Neel

Mauran's spiritual view of life has expanded her definition of the environment to include the interior landscapes of human beings, thus expanding the array of tools available to us to enact change in the world.

Mauran holds a bachelor of science in forestry from the University of New Hampshire. She founded Trees for Rye, a tree planting organization, and was a member of the Rye Conservation Commission. She has been a student of Biogeometry and of several wisdom traditions, including Hawaiian Temple Healing with Kahu Abraham Kawai'i and Harry Uhane Jim, Sadhguru Jaggi Vasudev's Isha Yoga, Ariel Spilsbury's Archetypal Journey Through the 13 Faces of the Divine Feminine and Craig Hamilton's Evolutionary Life Transformation Program, offered online by Integral Enlightenment.

Mauran has three children, a dog named Star, and lives in the Hudson Valley of New York state. She may be reached by email at Hope@ hopeivesmauran.com.

Bibliography

Beck, Don Edward, and Christopher C. Cowan. *Spiral Dynamics: Mastering Values, Leadership, and Change*. Malden, MA: Blackwell, 1996.

Calleman, Carl Johan. *The Mayan Calendar and the Transformation of Consciousness*. Rochester, VT: Bear & Company, 2004.

Cohen, Neil S. *Chakra Awareness Guide*. Mount Shasta, CA: AMI, 1989.

Epstein, Donald M. *The 12 Stages of Healing*. San Rafael, CA: Amber-Allen, 1994.

Garofalo, Michael. "A Victim Treats His Mugger Right." *Morning Edition. National Public Radio*. March 28, 2008. http://www.npr.org/templates/story/story.php?storyId=89164759&sc=emf.

Hamilton, Craig. "The Evolutionary Life Transformation Program" June 2010 to June 2011, San Rafael, CA: 2010. www.IntegralEnlightenment.com.

Hawkins, David R. *Transcending the Levels of Consciousness: The Stairway to Enlightenment*. West Sedona, AZ: Veritas, 2006.

Jenny, Hans. *Cymatics*. Newmarket, NH: MACROmedia, 2001.

Karim, Ibrahim. *Back to a Future for Mankind: Biogeometry Solutions to the Global Environmental Crisis.* Cairo, Egypt: Biogeometry Consulting, 2007–2009.

Karim, Ibrahim. Biogeometry Lectures. Sponsored by the Vesica Institute for Holistic Studies. Ashville, NC: November 2009.

Kilham, Christopher S., *The Five Tibetans: Five Dynamic Exercises for Health, Energy, and Personal Power.* Rochester, Vermont, Healing Arts Press, 1994.

Lewis, Dr. M. W., "Can Thought Change Matter?" Self-Realization Magazine, Fall 2004, Self Realization Fellowship.

Mauran, Hope Ives. *Where the Wisdom Lies: A Message from Nature's Small Creatures.* Bloomington, IN: AuthorHouse, 2006.

McTaggart, Lynne. *The Field: The Quest for the Secret Force of the Universe*, New York: HarperCollins, 2002.

Megre, Vladimir. *Anastasia.* Translated by Leonid Sharaskin. Ringing Cedars Series. Kahului, HI: Ringing Cedars Press, 2008.

Megre, Vladimir. *The Energy of Life.* Translated by Leonid Sharaskin. Ringing Cedars Series. Kahului, HI: Ringing Cedars Press, 2008.

Moore, Alanna. *Sensitive Permaculture: Cultivating the Way of the Sacred Earth.* Victoria, Aus.: Python, 2009.

Oespensky, P. D. *In Search of the Miraculous: Fragments of an Unknown Teaching.* New York: Harcourt Brace Jovanovich, 1949,

Rees, Camilla and Magda Havas. *Public Health SOS: The Shadow Side of the Wireless Revolution.* Boulder, CO: Wide Angle Health, 2009.

Saraswati, Swami Karmananda. "Mooladhara and Ajna: Two Poles of Energy." *Yoga Magazine.* March 1982. Retrieved May 8, 2010, from www.yogamag.net/archives/1982/cmar82/moolaj.shtml.

Saraswati, Swami Nishchalananda. *The Chakras: Keys to a Quantum Leap in Human Evolution.* Mandala Yoga Ashram: Wales, UK. Retrieved December 19, 2009, from http://www.mandalayoga.net/prettyprint-newsletter-en-chakras.html.

Scott, Steven K. *The Greatest Words Ever Spoken: Everything Jesus Said about You, Your Life, and Everything Else.* Colorado Springs, CO: Waterbrook, 2008.

Sharashkin, Leonid. Ringing Cedars Workshop. Sedona, AZ: Oct. 5–6, 2009.

Simmons, Robert, and Naisha Ahsian. *The Book of Stones.* Montpelier, VT: Heaven & Earth, 2007,

Spalding, Baird T. *Life and Teaching of the Masters of the Far East.* 6 vols. Marina del Rey, CA: DeVorss, 1972.

Whitefield, Patrick. *How to Make a Forest Garden.* Hampshire, Eng.: Permanent Publications, 2002.

Wilber, Ken. Talk for Evolutionary Life Transformation Program an on online class. Special Topics Lecture. Integral Enlightenment, San Rafael, California, December 2010.

Wilson, Colin. *Alien Dawn. A Classic Investigation into the Contact Experience.* Woodbury, MNL: Llewellyn, 2010.

Wright, Machaelle Small. *Behaving as If the God in All Things Mattered.* Jeffersonton, VA: Perelandra, 1997.

Yogananda, Paramahansa. *The Second Coming of Christ.* Vol. 1 of *The Resurrection of the Christ Within You.* Los Angeles, CA: Self-Realization Fellowship, 2004.

Yogananda, Paramahansa. *The Yoga of Jesus.* Los Angeles, CA: Self-Realization Fellowship, 2007.

Yogananda, Paramahansa, "An AuthenticGlimpse of Jesus' Divine Life", *Self-Realization Magazine*, Fall 2004, Self Realization Fellowship.

Endnotes

1. Yogananda, *The Second Coming of Christ,* 142.
2. Yogananda, *The Yoga of Jesus,* 5.

CPSIA information can be obtained at www.ICGtesting.com
Printed in the USA
BVOW031120041011

272731BV00001B/6/P